My
Spiritual
Inheritance

Companion Study Guide

My Spiritual Inheritance

Companion Study Guide

Juanita Bynum

Charisma
HOUSE
A STRANG COMPANY

Most Strang Communications/Charisma House/Siloam products
are available at special quantity discounts for bulk purchase for sales
promotions, premiums, fund-raising, and educational needs. For details,
write Strang Communications/Charisma House/Siloam, 600 Rinehart Road,
Lake Mary, Florida 32746, or telephone (407) 333-0600.

My Spiritual Inheritance Companion Study Guide by Juanita Bynum
Published by Charisma House
A Strang Company
600 Rinehart Road
Lake Mary, Florida 32746
www.charismahouse.com

Unless otherwise noted, all Scripture quotations are from the Amplified
Bible. Old Testament copyright © 1965, 1987 by the Zondervan
Corporation. The Amplified New Testament copyright © 1954, 1958, 1987
by the Lockman Foundation. Used by permission.

Scripture quotations marked KJV are from the King James Version of the
Bible.

Scripture quotations marked NIV are from the Holy Bible, New
International Version. Copyright © 1973, 1978, 1984, International Bible
Society. Used by permission.

Cover design by Judith McKittrick
Interior design by Terry Clifton

Copyright © 2005 by Juanita Bynum
All rights reserved
Library of Congress Control Number: 2004110393
International Standard Book Number: 1-59185-610-8

05 06 07 08 09 — 987654321
Printed in the United States of America

C O N T E N T S

About This Book

*T*his companion study guide has been designed to accompany my book *My Spiritual Inheritance*. You can benefit from it whether or not you have a copy of that book. It is designed to help you know when you have met your spiritual parents, to recognize when they are preparing you to receive your spiritual inheritance, and to show you how to guard against losing that inheritance.

In each chapter, you will find the following elements:

- Excerpts from the corresponding chapter in *My Spiritual Inheritance* to provide a framework for the Bible studies and questions
- Pertinent scriptures, including one that you might want to memorize
- Exercises of various types to help you think through and apply the ideas (You can write in this book.)
- An inspirational personal testimony
- "The Essentials"—a one-sentence summary of the main point of each chapter
- "To Your Father"—a powerful prayer to link you to your heavenly Father

You can use this book as a guide for small-group discussions, or you can study it all by yourself. Either way, you are linked with your brothers and sisters who belong to the Father.

Our Father's inheritance is so vast that there is more than enough for every believer. And yet each believer is as special as an only child, who receives the entire inheritance without splitting it with brothers and sisters.

Don't just study this book to learn concepts—*apply* the truths. I guarantee that you will find your destiny in God!

My Spiritual Inheritance

*Y*ou can have the experience of salvation and receive a new heart, but still miss the experience of receiving your spiritual inheritance—the portion from your heavenly Father that is supposed to be implanted into your new heart. Receiving your spiritual inheritance is an ongoing process. After you receive a new heart, your heart must be fed continually by your heavenly Father. Just as you need daily nourishment to keep your physical body alive, you need to be receiving your daily spiritual portion from your heavenly Father to reach your full potential in Christ—to inherit fully the spiritual portion that He has for you.

My Papa

I was raised in the church, but I never before really thought about whether or not I was receiving everything my heavenly Father intended for me to have as my spiritual inheritance. This lack of knowledge about His portion for me had robbed my life and hindered me from reaching my full potential in Him. I never understood how very relevant my relationship with my pastor was to my relationship with my heavenly Father. I never saw the association—until circumstances caused me to remember back to how I felt as a young teenager in Chicago when my first pastor, Luke Austin Sr., passed away. Everyone knew him as "Papa." Although his son, a profound teacher of the Word, took over the ministry, still I felt lost, disconnected. I began to wander spiritually.

Soon to be eighteen, I asked my mom for permission to move to Milwaukee, Wisconsin. I was searching for more, but I didn't know it. Papa Austin had been like a spiritual father to me, and I didn't understand the weight of his influence upon my life. My parents understood, but I hadn't come to terms with it.

I started searching for something, not knowing what I was searching for. Along the way, I came across several pastors, but it wasn't until 1982 when I moved to Port Huron, Michigan, that God gave me a man who would function as my next spiritual father. I knew it the moment I walked into the office of Pastor William and Sister Veter Nichols. God wanted me to receive the full portion of what He wanted to give me—and He wants you to receive the full portion of your spiritual inheritance, too.

> LORD, you have assigned me my portion and my cup;
> you have made my lot secure.
> The boundary lines have fallen for me in pleasant places;
> surely I have a delightful inheritance.
>
> —PSALM 16:5–6, NIV

The Full Portion

The Lord is my portion or share, says my living being (my inner self); therefore will I hope in Him and wait expectantly for Him. The Lord is good to those who wait hopefully and expectantly for Him, to those who seek Him [inquire of and for Him and require Him by right of necessity and on the authority of God's word].

—LAMENTATIONS 3:24–25

1. According to this passage of Scripture, what is your portion (your inheritance)?

2.   What are the two keys to unlocking your portion? (Find two
key verbs in verse 24.)

_____

_____

3.   Are these verbs active or passive? How can you tell from the
way they are used in the passage?

_____

_____

_____

A Word to Leaders

If you are a pastor or leader, this book will help you to recognize
the great responsibility we have as leaders to rise to a new level in
our own relationship with God so that we are able to impart God's
portion to the people who are coming to us for spiritual leadership.
A leader is accountable for speaking the Word of the Lord to the
congregation. When you stand in front of others, ask yourself, *Are
people receiving their portion, or are they just getting another message?* If they are receiving their portion from God through you,
then you are helping them to move into their destinies.

I believe a lot of people are asking, *Where is my spiritual inheritance?* It is God's desire to change the world one person at a
time. When a person walks into your ministry and sits under your
spiritual leadership, God's sole motive for that person is to birth
him or her into destiny through your leadership.

Feed My Sheep

When they had eaten, Jesus said to Simon Peter, Simon, son of John, do you love Me more than these [others do—with reasoning, intentional, spiritual devotion, as one loves the Father]? He said to Him, Yes, Lord, You know that I love You [that I have deep, instinctive, personal affection for You, as for a close friend]. He said to him, Feed My lambs. Again He said to him the second time, Simon, son of John, do you love Me [with reasoning, intentional, spiritual devotion, as one loves the Father]? He said to Him, Yes, Lord, You know that I love You [that I have a deep, instinctive, personal affection for You as for a close friend]. He said to him, Shepherd (tend) My sheep.

He said to him the third time, Simon, son of John, do you love Me [with a deep, instinctive, personal affection for Me, as for a close friend]? Peter was grieved (was saddened and hurt) that He should ask him the third time, Do you love Me? And he said to Him, Lord, You know everything; You know that I love You [that I have a deep, instinctive, personal affection for You, as for a close friend]. Jesus said to him, Feed My sheep.

—JOHN 21:15–17

If you are a pastor or a leader (which includes being a parent to your children), consider the following questions:

1.   When the Lord asked the question the first time, do you think that Peter felt sure that he loved his Lord with his whole heart? Why or why not?

_____

_____

2.   Why do you think Jesus asked him the same question three times?

_____

_____

_____

3.   Have you ever felt the pain, as Simon Peter did, of the Lord's probing inquiry? What was the result in your life?

_____

_____

4.   Why does the exhortation, "Feed My sheep" prove the depth of Peter's love? Why did the Lord not say instead, "Fall down in adoration before Me," or "Rejoice in the revelations I show you"? What is so deep about feeding His sheep?

_____

_____

_____

5.   As a pastor, many people in your congregation or group are not yet in possession of their spiritual inheritance. Do you realize that they rely on your strength? (You are the one they can see and hear.) Do you accept the fact that your role can be very tiring as people draw from you? What can you do to be sure that your "well" doesn't run dry?

_____

_____

_____

Posture of Believers

If you are the one seeking spiritual leadership and nourishment in the body of Christ, your connection to a local ministry should be based upon a divine relationship that you have with the leadership of that local ministry. Your connection to that church should not be based upon the choir or the praise and worship team, not upon the basketball club or the usher's board, and not because you like the fact that they throw big birthday parties for their members. In short, you should not join a church for the activities.

Too many people have done this. They haven't linked to the divine portion of their spiritual fathers and the deposit of their spiritual mothers. People come to church, but their hearts are not in the right posture.

> My son, hear the instruction of your father; reject not nor forsake the teaching of your mother. For they are a [victor's] chaplet (garland) of grace upon your head and chains and pendants [of gold worn by kings] for your neck.
>
> —Proverbs 1:8–9

Leaders have been called to feed, which means *you must eat.* The Bible's pattern is clear—spiritual leaders are to lead, and we are to submit under their spiritual leadership for spiritual direction.

The Father's portion is a meal that satisfies, and it must be digested in order to work in our lives. So when we walk through the doors of the church, it's time for a feeding. We should come prepared to worship the Father and to receive a meal from His table. The best time to eat isn't when you're starving—because you'll eat anything then. Too many of us in the body of Christ are starving because we only eat a healthy meal once or twice a week. In other words, we don't maintain intimacy with God on a daily basis, so we can't even digest properly what we receive from Him. We are malnourished.

To receive from the Father, you must first be able to acknowledge that God can give your leader the ability to see into your life and to tap into the Spirit. Trust must be developed. But just because you don't have a bond of trust with your leader does not necessarily mean that you need to change churches. *You may simply need to change your posture.* That's what I did. And when I changed, the Spirit of the Lord made sure that I didn't miss out on receiving my spiritual inheritance.

Are You Hungry?

1. Are you getting good spiritual nourishment?

_____

2. Can you determine why or why not?

_____

_____

3. Are you aware of good spiritual nourishment that is within your grasp if you exerted the effort to obtain it? Where is it?

_____

_____

_____

4. Do the brothers and sisters around you have good spiritual food to "eat"? Why or why not?

_____

_____

_____

The Essentials

God wants you to receive the full portion of your spiritual inheritance.

I pray also that the eyes of your heart may be enlightened in order that you may know the hope to which he has called you, the riches of his glorious inheritance in the saints, and his incomparably great power for us who believe.
—Ephesians 1:18–19, NIV

To Your Father

Father, I read in Your Word [James 1:5] that if I lack wisdom, all I have to do is ask You for it, and You will grant it to me. I do lack wisdom about my spiritual inheritance, so I ask for wisdom about this.

I know that You are my heavenly Father, and You are the Giver of inheritance. Open my mind and my heart to receive from You as I read this book and study Your Word. Show me how to adopt a posture that is ready to receive from Your hand. Keep me humble and hungry, even as You satisfy me. Thank You. Amen.

CHAPTER 1

The Voice of the Father

When I moved to Port Huron, Michigan, it was the beginning of an intense, nine-year process of spiritual growth. At the time, I was young in the Lord and immature in the Spirit. I needed the mentorship of my new spiritual parents, Pastor William and Sister Veter Nichols. I actually called them *Mom* and *Dad*, because that's what we normally did in church. Even still, I didn't truly embrace the portion the Father was trying to give me.

God was trying to impart a new level of revelation in my spirit. He was introducing me to His order, but I couldn't see it because of things that were going on in my life. I was battling a lot of emotional issues and had my own ideas about what I wanted to do. As a result, the Nichols had to correct me constantly. At the time, I didn't understand the power and anointing that were being imparted to me with every correction, and I left Port Huron before it was time for me to go, making a move to New York City. You can read the full story about my decision to leave in my book *No More Sheets.*

I ran into some bad situations. Ultimately, I had to call Pastor Nichols and repent. I had to ask for his forgiveness because I had walked out from under his leadership in a spirit of rebellion. He received my apology and, in turn, prayed with me that God would lead me to a church.

And you say, How I hated instruction and discipline, and my heart despised reproof! I have not obeyed the voice of my teachers nor submitted and consented to those who instructed me.

—PROVERBS 5:12–13

Spiritual Parents and Children

I will not burden you [financially], for it is not your [money] that I want but you; for children are not duty bound to lay up store for their parents, but parents for their children. But I will most gladly spend [myself] and be utterly spent for your souls.

—2 CORINTHIANS 12:14–15

Paul was a spiritual father to the believers in Corinth.

1. In terms of providing for children, how is a spiritual father like the father of a family?

_____

_____

2. Is it possible for a child to earn his or her own living all alone, without help?

_____

3. A financial inheritance is conveyed to a child in one of two ways: either someone dies (usually a parent or one of our elders), or that person decides to give the child the funds beforehand. In what way does the bestowal of a spiritual inheritance follow the same pattern?

_____

_____

4.   What part does the child play in receiving an inheritance? (Think about what position the child must occupy.)

_____

_____

5.   Have you ever had a spiritual father (or mother)? Write down the name or names.

_____

6.   Do you have a spiritual father now?

_____

7.   Are you growing into the role of a spiritual father (or mother) yourself?

_____

There Is a Portion for You

When I think about this, I realize how awesome our God is. When you really belong to the Lord, when you're a child of the King, it becomes the Father's responsibility to make sure you get your spiritual inheritance. It is His responsibility to make sure you don't miss it. So even though I messed up in one sense, I didn't miss His portion for me through that experience. He is the God of the second chance—and that's exactly what He gave me.

When I arrived in New York, I was impoverished in my spirit and in my bank account. In my room, I would leave my radio tuned to a gospel station. Music would play for a couple of hours, and then there would be preaching. When I heard Dr. John H. Boyd Sr. speak for the first time, the power of God literally came through that radio. There was something about his voice that made me feel like I was back at home during my early days in Chicago.

Something quickened in me. My spirit identified with the sound of his voice even though, technically, he didn't sound like Papa Austin. It was something more than just his voice. In the Spirit realm it was a sound I recognized, the sound of impartation with the sense of comfort I had felt during those early years.

After that, while working as a flight attendant with Pan American Airlines, I listened to Dr. Boyd's radio programs. God is so faithful. I was in a new city, traveling all the time, yet God was introducing and connecting me in the Spirit realm to my spiritual inheritance through the man who would become my new spiritual father.

As a flight attendant I traveled all the time. I would walk into a hotel room, turn on the radio, and scan for a gospel station. On more than ten occasions, as soon as I located a gospel station, I heard "The Voice of Bethel" broadcast with Dr. John Boyd. When Dr. Boyd's words came through my radio, they went into my spirit. It seemed that everywhere I went, the Spirit of the Lord was making sure I didn't miss my Father's feeding. For six months, God continued this process of connecting me with my new spiritual father on earth.

> Just think of Him Who endured from sinners such grievous opposition and bitter hostility against Himself [reckon up and consider it all in comparison with your trials], so that you may not grow weary or exhausted, losing heart and relaxing and fainting in your minds.... You must submit to and endure [correction] for discipline; God is dealing with you as with sons. For what son is there whom his father does not [thus] train and correct and discipline?... Shall we not much more cheerfully submit to the Father of spirits and so [truly] live? For [our earthly fathers] disciplined us for only a short period of time and chastised us as seemed proper and good to them; but He disciplines us for our certain good, that we may become sharers in His own holiness.
>
> —HEBREWS 12:3, 7, 9–10

There Is a Portion for You

The experiences we have with our earthly fathers affect our ability to receive from our spiritual fathers. Some people have good, positive experiences with their fathers. Others have negative, even abusive, experiences. Some never knew their fathers.

1.   Write a few sentences about your earthly father. In what ways was he a good father? In what ways was he not?

_____

_____

_____

_____

2.   Has your experience of your earthly father made it easier or harder to receive your heavenly inheritance?

☐ Easier   ☐ Harder

3.   If you checked "Easier," take a moment to thank your heavenly Father and ask Him to bestow His blessings on you.

4.   If you checked "Harder," take a moment to ask God to begin to work in you to clear away the impediments to receiving blessings from Him. You might start by asking Him to help you forgive your earthly father for the ways in which he failed to give you what you needed.

Regardless of your experience with your earthly father, your heavenly Father will make sure that you experience His divine fatherhood. This is His gift to each of us.

Appointment With Destiny

One cold, winter Sunday morning in New York City [see "Getting Personal"], I parked my car and walked into Dr. Boyd's church for the first time. He was already preaching his message. Not even ten minutes into his sermon, he looked out into the audience directly at me and said, "Little lady, right there in that uniform. I don't know who you are or where you come from. But God told me that you're an eagle with broken wings, and there's a ministry down inside of you. Your worst days are behind you, and your best days are yet to come."

Without even a human touch, the power of God knocked me to the floor. When I got up, I said to the Lord, "I'm going to know I'm in the right place if, when I walk up to that offering table, the man of God says anything else to me."

The offering music started, and the people started going up to the offering table, row by row, starting from the back. When the ushers got to me, I was ready. With my $5.00 offering in my hand, I started making my way to the table. As I walked down the aisle, the pastor came down from the pulpit to the lowest step behind the offering baskets. As I was putting my offering in the basket, he reached out, grabbed my hand, and said, "Welcome to Bethel."

"OK, this is it," I said to the Lord. "This is where You've placed me."

Getting Personal

In order to initiate His divine plan for my life, God turned a frustrating situation into an appointment with destiny:

One Sunday morning, I woke up around 4:00 a.m. because I needed to get ready for work. My flight schedule read, "6:45 report." I got dressed and headed for the airport, planning to arrive, as usual, about an hour before crew check-in. By 6:45 I was walking into the

Pan American briefing room. The purser (lead flight attendant) came in and started reading the names of all the crew to make sure everybody was present. When she had read all of the names, she looked at me and said, "Who are you?"

"I'm Juanita Bynum."

"You're not on my list," she said.

I explained to her that my schedule had told me to report in at 6:45 a.m.

"Are you sure?" she asked.

"I have it right here…" I pulled the paper out of my purse, and it said 6:45 a.m. So we called the supervisor of scheduling, and he said, "That was a misprint. You don't report until 6:45 p.m." So, after getting all the way to the airport, I had to turn around and head back home. Needless to say, I was frustrated.

That particular morning, the temperature outside was below zero. When I was one block from home, I noticed a lady standing at a bus stop with three little kids. They were all bundled up. The Spirit of the Lord said, "Turn around, and ask that lady if she needs a ride."

So I turned around in obedience to God. I pulled up to the curb and offered her a ride, and, after a minute, she accepted. She was on her way to church.

When we pulled up to the church, I wasn't really paying attention to the sign in front. "This is where you go to church?"

"Yeah," she said.

"What is the name of your church?" I asked.

"New Greater Bethel."

The blood rushed to my face. "New Greater Bethel!" I exclaimed. "Dr. John H. Boyd Sr.?"

"Yes! That's my pastor."

"This Is the Way, Walk Ye in It"

And therefore will the Lord wait, that he may be gracious unto you, and therefore will he be exalted, that he may have mercy upon you: for the Lord is a God of judgment: blessed are all they that wait for him....thou shalt weep no more: he will be very gracious unto thee at the voice of thy cry; when he shall hear it, he will answer thee. And though the Lord give you the bread of adversity, and the water of affliction, yet shall not thy teachers be removed into a corner any more, but thine eyes shall see thy teachers: And thine ears shall hear a word behind thee, saying, This is the way, walk ye in it, when ye turn to the right hand, and when ye turn to the left.

—Isaiah 30:18–21, KJV

1.   According to this passage, what key action must you do to release God's gracious help?

_____

_____

2.   In your own life, how have you seen God's longing to bless you, even in the midst of adversity?

_____

_____

3.   Bread (of adversity) and water (of affliction) signify the food of a person who is in prison. In your own life, how have you tasted prisoner's food?

_____

_____

4.   For Isaiah, "thy teachers" would have been the prophets, such as Isaiah himself, whose words we now have in the Bible. There are

modern-day "teacher" counterparts in the men and women who speak God's Word. Put the following promise into your own words, applying it to your own life and including the "teachers" you can name:

> And though the Lord give you the bread of adversity, and the water of affliction, yet shall not thy teachers be removed into a corner any more, but thine eyes shall see thy teachers.
>
> —ISAIAH 30:20

Even though the Lord may give me...

_____

_____

_____

5.   How is God's guidance ("this is the way, walk ye in it") an expression of His mercy toward you, even though it is not something you can touch or taste or deposit in the bank?

_____

_____

_____

Come Out of the Wilderness

From the time I left Port Huron until the time God led me to that Sunday morning service at Dr. Boyd's church, I felt as though I had been wandering in a spiritual desert. No doubt you have experienced your own spiritual wilderness.

Your Wilderness Experience

Are you walking in some kind of a spiritual wilderness right now? Evaluate your circumstances:

1. Do you feel like you're not being fed anymore?

   Yes ☐ No ☐

2. Do you wish you had better spiritual food?

   Yes ☐ No ☐

3. Are your "streams" dry or bitter?

   Yes ☐ No ☐

4. Do you grumble that you used to be better off?

   Yes ☐ No ☐

5. Read what God told the Israelites in Exodus 14:14. Put His advice into your own words for your own situation:

_____

_____

_____

_____

When Pharaoh let the people go, God led them not by way of the land of the Philistines, although that was nearer; for God said, Lest the people change their purpose when they see war and return to Egypt. But God led the people around by way of the wilderness toward the Red Sea.

—Exodus 13:17–18

I believe a wilderness experience is a journey to find our spiritual fathers. The children of Israel wandered in the wilderness until they found the divine place. Egypt wasn't it. Egypt had been their place of bondage. *Remember this:* Any place where you are not receiving the manifold blessings of God is your spiritual Egypt.

The Israelites belonged to their heavenly Father. Because they were His chosen children, God was obligated to get them out of Egypt. He had a divine place for them—*Canaan*—but they had to go through the wilderness before they reached it. You know the story.

The vast majority of that first generation never made it to the Promised Land because they were disobedient. A few, however, were brought into their destiny. Joshua and Caleb became leaders for the next generation. They reached the Promised Land.

If you have received Jesus and are still going through a *wilderness experience,* be confident that you belong to God. As long as you obey Him, God will make sure you receive His portion.

The Essentials

It is the Father's responsibility to make sure you get your spiritual inheritance.

Memory Verse

Praise be to the God and Father of our Lord Jesus Christ! In his great mercy he has given us new birth into a living hope through the resurrection of Jesus Christ from the dead, and into an inheritance that can never perish, spoil or fade.

—1 PETER 1:3–4, NIV

To Your Father

Father, I am believing that You want me to come into my full inheritance. But I'm unsure of the next steps I need to take. [Write down a few of the questions you would like God to answer for you.]

_____

_____

_____

_____

I trust that You have heard my heart and that, as I wait expectantly over the next period of time, You will be answering my questions and showing me how to take the next steps. In the name of Jesus I pray, amen.

CHAPTER 2

The Power of Obedience

When God gives you a spiritual father or mother, then you want to show appreciation to God by becoming a servant in that person's house. In other words, when you are in the house of your spiritual father, you are not content with being simply a bench member.

Your Portion Is Your Measure

Our desire to build the kingdom of God comes because the heavenly Father has imparted to each of us a "measure" of faith. When you receive God, you automatically receive this impartation. You also receive specific spiritual gifts that are meant to help you build the kingdom of God. (See Romans 12:4–8.)

> For by the grace (unmerited favor of God) given to me I warn everyone among you not to estimate and think of himself more highly than he ought [not to have an exaggerated opinion of his own importance], but to rate his ability with sober judgment, each according to the degree of faith apportioned by God to him.
>
> —Romans 12:3

At the moment of conversion, you were given faith and spiritual gifts with which to build God's kingdom. Whatever the vision of your father is, you have been equipped with the spirit of a servant, a calling, gifts, and talents that correspond to his vision. The anointing you have is not for you. It is to fulfill the vision your heavenly Father has given to your spiritual father and mother.

The whole purpose of Jesus' life was to finish the work of His Father (John 4:34). Jesus has extended this assignment to us. Just as He is responsible to the Father, so your responsibility is to help fulfill the vision, desires, and assignment that God has given to your spiritual father. Your measure is your spiritual assignment.

Many Christians don't have a revelation of this. We think our job is simply to sing in the choir or to be an usher. We don't understand that we are an intricate part of the puzzle that moves a vision forward and causes it to flourish.

The Father didn't give you a partial measure. The *degree* of your faith is a full measure.

> If you keep My commandments [if you continue to obey My instructions], you will abide in My love and live on in it, just as I have obeyed My Father's commandments and live on in His love. I have told you these things, that my joy and delight may be in you, and that your joy and gladness may be of full measure and complete and overflowing.
>
> —John 15:10–11

Getting Personal

When I joined New Greater Bethel, the manifestation of the servant spirit in me was a sign that I was home. I knew that I'd met the spiritual father my heavenly Father had prepared for me, because I had an immediate desire to serve in a place I'd never been before. My first reaction wasn't, "I don't know these people; I don't know this building; I don't know this church or anything about it." Instead, my immediate response to God was, *"What can I do? Can I sweep, mop, or staple papers? Can I do something to help?"*

From the time I started attending Bethel, I was being driven by the measure of faith He had given me. I trusted in God's supernatural provision, and I believed He had bestowed upon me a new spiritual father. Immediately, I wanted to do whatever I could to build His kingdom through my church. I wanted God's kingdom to become great because of what I had been given.

There Is Power in Obedience

Whatever you believe God is calling you to accomplish as an individual is part of a spiritual vision that is being passed from generation to generation.

Jesus didn't come to start His own dynasty. He came to build His Father's kingdom, to fulfill His Father's vision. Everything Jesus said and did referred people back to the Father. He didn't want the praise for Himself. He performed miracles and said, "Don't tell anybody." He was on earth to complete an assignment from His Father, and He didn't want His Father's glory.

When Jesus finished fulfilling the plan of His Father, He moved out of the way and sent the baptism of the Holy Spirit to His followers. Now His followers would be fulfilling the vision of the Father. As a man, Jesus could be in only one town at a time, performing one miracle at a time. Now He has released Himself to live inside every person who believes in Him, throughout history and throughout the world. What this means is that *we* are finishing His work—His work is to finish His Father's work. When we submit to our spiritual parents, it's so much deeper than just "He's my pastor" or "She's my pastor." We are part of a greater vision.

Jesus was obedient to the Father when He accepted His assignment. But He had to learn further obedience in the same way that we do. Hebrews 5:8–9 says, "Although He was a Son, He learned [active, special] obedience through what He suffered. And, [His completed experience] making Him perfectly [equipped], He became the

Author and Source of eternal salvation to all those who give heed and obey Him." Jesus is constantly speaking out, "Let Me show you the way to power. You get power through the things you suffer." But the church tries to escape from pain and discomfort.

We have not learned obedience through what we have suffered. And we have no power because we have no obedience.

> You have commanded us to keep Your precepts, that we should observe them diligently. Oh, that my ways were directed and established to observe Your statutes [hearing, receiving, loving, and obeying them]! Then shall I not be put to shame [by failing to inherit Your promises] when I have respect to all Your commandments.
>
> —PSALM 119:4–6

Don't Miss the Punctuation

Peter, an apostle (a special messenger) of Jesus Christ, [writing] to the elect exiles of the dispersion scattered (sowed) abroad in Pontus, Galatia, Cappadocia, Asia, and Bithynia, who were chosen and foreknown by God the Father and consecrated (sanctified, made holy) by the Spirit to be obedient to Jesus Christ (the Messiah) and to be sprinkled with [His] blood:

May grace (spiritual blessing) and peace be given you in increasing abundance [that spiritual peace to be realized in and through Christ, freedom from fears, agitating passions, and moral conflicts]. Praised (honored, blessed) be the God and Father of our Lord Jesus Christ (the Messiah)! By His boundless mercy we have been born again to an ever-living hope through the resurrection of Jesus Christ from the dead.

[Born anew] into an inheritance which is beyond

the reach of change and decay [imperishable], unsullied and unfading, reserved in heaven for you, who are being guarded (garrisoned) by God's power through [your] faith [till you fully inherit that final] salvation that is ready to be revealed [for you] in the last time.

—1 PETER 1:1–5

(Note the colon at the end of the first paragraph above. It means that whatever is stated after the colon is dependent upon that which was stated before it. In other words, there are "pre-colon" spiritual steps that need to be taken before we can move past the colon to the blessings.)

1.   Make a list of the "post-colon" blessings that are guaranteed to us if we fulfill the "pre-colon" requirements. You should be able to find at least four blessings:

_____

_____

_____

2.   Who makes us able to fulfill the "pre-colon" requirements?

_____

3.   What is the purpose of our being "chosen" and "consecrated"?

_____

_____

4.   We possess something that enables God's power to guard these blessings for us. What is it? ("Guarded by God's power through _____.")

_____

Don't Get Disgruntled

One reason the body of Christ hasn't yet reached the purpose of doing the Father's will is because we stay so offended. We don't understand that the only way we can prove that we are the authentic body of Christ is to have scars. We have to have nail prints. To be authentic sons and daughters, we have to be whipped, spat upon, and talked about.

Because you belong to the body of Christ, you will have to walk through difficult situations, deal with hard issues—and survive. You survive by activating your "measure of faith." As you do so, the most important part of you is being renewed, the spiritual part that fulfills the kingdom-building plan of the Father.

> I am fearful that somehow or other I may come and find you not as I desire to find you, and that you may find me too not as you want to find me—that perhaps there may be factions (quarreling), jealousy, temper (wrath, intrigues, rivalry, divided loyalties), selfishness, whispering, gossip, arrogance (self-assertion), and disorder among you.
> —2 Corinthians 12:20

Don't get offended or disgruntled at the vision of your spiritual father. You have become one piece of the puzzle that he was commissioned to oversee. Every vision that God has given to His leaders is part of the puzzle. There are no two churches alike. Remember this when you wish your church had a soup kitchen. Maybe God hasn't called your church to have a soup kitchen! He may have called the ministry across town to do that.

The Great Must Serve Others

But Jesus called them *[all of the disciples]* to [Him] and said to them, You know that those who are recognized as governing and are supposed to rule the Gentiles (the nations) lord it over them [ruling with absolute power, holding them in subjection], and their great men exercise authority and dominion over them. But this is not to be so among you; instead, whoever desires to be great among you must be your servant, and whoever wishes to be most important and first in rank among you must be slave of all. For even the Son of Man came not to have service rendered to Him, but to serve, and to give His life as a ransom for (instead of) many.

—Mark 10:42–45

1. Within the past 24 hours, have you served someone else voluntarily?

_____

2. Did you receive any immediate reward for your work?

_____

3. If so, what was it?

_____

_____

_____

4. What invisible reward might follow your service?

_____

_____

_____

5.   Have you adopted the posture of a servant within your church?

_____

6.   How do you see this kind of servanthood modeled by the people around you?

_____

_____

_____

7.   How do your leaders serve others?

_____

_____

_____

8.   Read Luke 16:12. What additional reason for being faithful in serving others do you find in this verse?

_____

_____

Coming Into Spiritual Order

God's way always involves a process of coming through something in order to get to Him. He built the temple structure so the people of Israel would have to come through the East Gate in order to come into the outer court, after which they could enter the holy place, which was located before the holy of holies. (See Exodus 25–27.) The people had to go through something to get to the next place.

When you obey God, you are acknowledging the authority of the process He has established. God perfectly designed the plan of salvation through Jesus: "No man cometh unto the Father, but by me" (John 14:6, KJV). We need to walk in spiritual order.

God didn't send the children of Israel rampaging out of Egypt. He gave them a leader to get them out. And when that leader disobeyed Him, He gave them another leader to take them into the Promised Land. *Leading is God's way.*

We have trouble with this idea. It makes us uncomfortable. Sometimes we exchange the leader God has sent for an image. We diminish the revelation and word of God that comes from our pastor by exchanging it for an image in a nice suit with a nice office and a title. When we do this, we keep wandering, never reaching our divine destiny. We can go to church every Sunday and still be wandering in a spiritual wilderness.

When you don't want to listen to the direction your pastor gives you because you think you know better, you are like the Israelites. Every time the Israelites got into rebellion, they said, "Moses, tell us what God is saying." But other times they said, "We want to talk to God ourselves."

Today everybody is saying, "I'm hearing from God." You're not hearing from God if you are in rebellion. God gives us only what we can handle—our leaders. God is saying, "If you can't handle *that* person, then you can't handle Me. If you can't find Me in your leader, you can't find Me by yourself."

God's way is the leader way. From the beginning to the end of the Bible, God has always used a leader to bring victory to His people. In essence, every leader walks under the same principle as every son and daughter. Nobody escapes the process of obedience and submission. When you submit to authority in obedience to God, then you have the power to command the enemy. If you are going to accomplish anything for God, you have to be in divine order.

When you comply in obedience with someone else's wishes and orders, you are covered. When God has given someone the right to make decisions that cover you, and you respect the authority that has been placed over your life, you have direction and protection. Because your leader stands higher in the Spirit realm, his vision is broader. He can order the enemy out of your life. He can unlock your destiny.

It may be the case that you don't have a spiritual leader. Then you're like the Israelites when they reached the Red Sea. You are at the end of your road and can't go any further. The reason you're not crossing over, while the enemy is behind you jumping all over your back, tearing up your house, your marriage, and your children, is that you don't have a leader to hold his hands up on your behalf. Too many believers don't have spiritual fathers.

> Obey your spiritual leaders and submit to them [continually recognizing their authority over you], for they are constantly keeping watch over your souls and guarding your spiritual welfare, as men who will have to render an account [of their trust]. [Do your part to] let them do this with gladness and not with sighing and groaning, for that would not be profitable to you [either].
>
> —Hebrews 13:17

Divine Order

Whether they are leaders or followers or both, people can become independent and may think they can do whatever they want.

Look up the following verses, which describe specific, decisive words and actions. Some of the words were spoken in obedience to God's will, and they display His divine order. The other words were spoken from an independent spirit—the results of those decisions display *dis*order.

Put a "O" (for *obedient*) on the line next to the examples of God's divine order.

Put a "I" (for *independent*) on the line next to the examples of human independence from God's order.

_____ **Exodus 14:15–22**

_____ **Numbers 12:1–15**

_____ **1 Samuel 1:16–20**

_____ **1 Samuel 15**

_____ **1 Chronicles 21:1–7**

_____ **Luke 22:49–51**

_____ **Acts 5:1–6**

_____ **Acts 10**

The Principle of Satan

When Satan was still called *Lucifer*, he was in the heavenlies serving God. He was a worshiper; that's what he was created to do. But he wanted to become equal with God. He said, "I will ascend to heaven; I will exalt my throne above the stars of God.…I will make myself like the Most High" (Isa. 14:13–14). The minute Lucifer began the whole *"I"* thing, he became an individual without God.

The power of the Godhead is in the Trinity: Father, Son, and Holy Spirit. The conversation of Christ is always, "We, Us, and Our." So the minute you cancel out God and start saying, "I…I…I," you diminish yourself back to the flesh realm, and you are disconnected from the Source of power. And the only thing the flesh can do is die. That means your ministry will die; everything that you operate in will die as long as you're saying "I."

Although Lucifer didn't mind worshiping God, he would not submit to God. Any time we disobey God, we are operating under the same principle, the principle of Satan. The principle of Satan is running rampant in the church today. We worship God, we preach, we prophesy, and we pray—but we won't obey.

Disobedience is rebellion, and the Bible says that rebellion is "as the sin of witchcraft" (1 Sam. 15:23).

The enemy isn't afraid of a person who preaches. He's not scared of the person who's shouting and speaking in tongues in church. He's not even threatened by someone who can quote the Bible verbatim from cover to cover. But he is terrified of the person who has submitted his life under the obedience of Christ. Satan is petrified of obedience.

After being born again, you are part of the body of Christ. "Born again" comes with both the desire and power to obey. If you are constantly walking in disobedience, then the plan of salvation is missing from your life. When God says, "Go left," do you go right? When God says, "Be quiet," do you talk? When God says, "Fast," do you eat? When God says, "Pray," do you watch television?

You don't need a word from the Lord. You need to obey. You don't need to pray for peace, because peace comes with obedience. You don't need to pray for abundance, because it comes with obedience. You don't have to pray for favor or protection, because they come with obedience. The question remains: are you really submitted?

The Essentials

True sons and daughters in the kingdom are focused on the will and vision of their spiritual fathers. We are empowered by obedience and submission.

Memory Verse

I have been crucified with Christ and I no longer live, but Christ lives in me. The life I live in the body, I live by faith in the Son of God, who loved me and gave himself for me.

—GALATIANS 2:20, NIV

To Your Father

My Father, forgive me for becoming disgruntled with the decisions of the leaders You have given me. [Ask Him to forgive you for whatever else may have come to the surface as you worked on this chapter.]

_____

_____

_____

Because of the measure of faith You have given me, I am able to believe that You have enabled me to ask for forgiveness, and You will carry me the rest of the way into true freedom. I ask You, Lord, to accomplish Your purposes in me. [Complete this prayer by writing the prayer that is in your heart.]

_____

_____

_____

Because of Jesus, amen.

CHAPTER 3

Receiving the Father's Portion

*I*n the story of Samuel anointing Saul as the first king of Israel, we can see a pattern for receiving the Father's portion, our spiritual inheritance. You can read about it in the ninth chapter of the Book of 1 Samuel. If you think back to the beginning of your life in Christ, most likely you will find that you followed the same pattern as Saul.

First of all, Saul started out as a nobody. He was the son of a man named Kish, of the little tribe of Benjamin. He was very handsome, but he hadn't done anything great. As the story begins, Saul was going with a servant to look for lost donkeys, in obedience to his father. He and the servant stayed out so long that finally he said to the servant, "Maybe we ought to go back so my father won't worry about us." (See verses 3–5.) But his servant said, "Behold now, there is in this city a man of God, a man held in honor; all that he says surely comes true. Now let us go there. Perhaps he can show us where we should go" (1 Sam. 9:6).

The servant understood authority, and he made sure that the son kept walking in obedience to his father's wishes. When Saul was ready to give up, the servant said, "Let's keep looking for the donkeys; let's ask for help." (If Saul had given up his search and had returned to his father, they would not have found Samuel. He may not have encountered the spiritual father who could lead him into his spiritual inheritance.)

So they went up to the city, and as they were entering, behold, Samuel came toward them, going up to the high place. Now a day before Saul came, the Lord had revealed to Samuel in his ear, Tomorrow about this time I will send you a man from the land of Benjamin, and you shall anoint him to be leader over My people Israel; and he shall save them out of the hand of the Philistines. For I have looked upon the distress of My people, because their cry has come to Me.

—1 SAMUEL 9:14–16

Understand this about spiritual relationships: before you get there, the man or woman of God already knows who you are in the Spirit. Saul came looking for donkeys, but God wanted to anoint him king of Israel.

Entering Into Purpose

Saul came looking for donkeys, but God had already shown Samuel Saul was going to deliver Israel from her enemies. God's call is greater than donkeys. Hear me. Your call is greater than what you think. Whether you play the piano, sing on the worship team, or are starting up a soup kitchen, your calling is significant. But you can't see it.

The man or woman of God can anoint you for your purpose. You can't do it! You can't even find the donkeys by yourself. You don't have enough discernment in your spirit to know where they are.

The principle reveals obedience in operation. Saul was obedient to his father, looking for donkeys. Samuel was obedient to his heavenly Father, who told him, "Tomorrow, look for this man, because you have to anoint him." If Samuel had disobeyed God and had gone up to eat without waiting for Saul to come to him, there would have been no King Saul. And without King Saul, there would be no King David. And without David, there would be no lineage for Christ to be born into the world.

When your spiritual leader is introduced to you, that leader will not be surprised by who you are. Samuel was not surprised by

Saul. We read: "When Samuel saw Saul, the Lord told him, There is the man of whom I told you. He shall have authority over My people. Then Saul came near to Samuel in the gate and said, Tell me where is the seer's house?" (1 Sam. 9:17–18). Did you catch that? Saul was staring the seer in the face and didn't have enough discernment to recognize him!

When Christians go from church to church looking for their spiritual parents but cannot find them, it is because they don't have the spiritual discernment to recognize who their spiritual parents really are. They don't value their leaders, because their spiritual eyesight isn't mature enough to discern what a spiritual parent could mean to their lives. They see their pastor as just a man in a suit.

Saul was looking straight at the seer, asking him, "Where is the seer?" Samuel answered, "I am the seer. Go up before me to the high place, for you shall eat with me today, and tomorrow I will let you go and will tell you all that is on your mind" (vv. 18–19). These verses reveal two important spiritual principles about your spiritual father. How do you know who is to be your future spiritual father? Two ways: (1) You will eat what he feeds you, and (2) he will be able to discern your spirit. It does not matter what kind of image you try to show to your spiritual father. It doesn't matter how hard you try to convince him of your spiritual depth or power. He has discernment about you already. He will confirm what is in your spirit—because he will be able to identify the real you.

> And now [brethren], I commit you to God [I deposit you in His charge, entrusting you to His protection and care]. And I commend you to the Word of His grace [to the commands and counsels and promises of His unmerited favor]. It is able to build you up and to give you [your rightful] inheritance among all God's set-apart ones (those consecrated, purified, and transformed of soul).
>
> —Acts 20:32

Hannah

Read the first chapter of 1 Samuel, the story of Hannah, the mother of the seer Samuel.

1. When he saw her in the temple, how did the priest Eli err in respect to Hannah?

_____

_____

2. Did this disqualify him from being Hannah's spiritual father, the one through whom her prayers would be answered?

_____

3. Do you think that Hannah found it easy to give Samuel up to the care of Eli? Why or why not?

_____

_____

In whom was she trusting?

_____

4. Who became Samuel's spiritual father?

_____

5. In spite of the short time that Hannah cared for her son Samuel in her home, she seems to have modeled for him a pattern of obedient trust in God. How do you think she did this?

_____

_____

Discovering True Riches

Samuel didn't fail to address the matter of Saul's lost donkeys. He said to Saul, "As for your donkeys that were lost three days ago, do not be thinking about them, for they are found" (1 Sam. 9:20). There can be a parallel experience for us when we meet our spiritual parents. When I met Pastor and Sister Nichols in Port Huron, they told me things about myself that I hadn't said to anyone. The same thing happened when I met Pastor Boyd at New Greater Bethel Ministries. He started to speak things about me that he couldn't have known in the natural because he didn't know me.

After confirming to Saul that his father's donkeys had been found, Samuel raised Saul's vision to the bigger picture of his spiritual inheritance. In the same way, a spiritual father raises your vision. As with Saul, your thinking moves from donkeys to destiny. When your spiritual father finds you, he will anoint you to receive victory over everything that threatens to hurt your family or to destroy your lineage.

As you are introduced to your destiny, your life will take a turn. Saul felt insufficient. He responded to Samuel, "Am I not a Benjamite, of the smallest of the tribes of Israel? And is not my family the least of all the families of the clans of Benjamin? Why then do you speak this way to me?" (v. 21). The man of God was speaking to Saul that way not because his family was renowned, but because he was going to give his family something they had never had. God had already set aside his portion, both his portion of choice meat for the meal and his spiritual portion.

> And He raised us up together with Him and made us sit down together [giving us joint seating with Him] in the heavenly sphere [by virtue of our being] in Christ Jesus (the Messiah, the Anointed One). He did this that He might clearly demonstrate through the ages to come the immeasurable (limitless, surpassing) riches of His free

grace (His unmerited favor) in [His] kindness and goodness of heart toward us in Christ Jesus.

—EPHESIANS 2:6–7

Getting Personal

When I first moved away from home, I tried to find
a church. I would go to one for a while, then decide that
something about it just wasn't quite a fit for me. More or
less by default, I finally ended up at a big church I could
walk to from my apartment. I felt that the spiritual atmosphere was inadequate, so I began to look for a Bible
study to attend.

There was an older woman in the church who had
taught a Bible study for a long time. The people in it used
to be all women about her age, but the young adults in the
church were starting to attend, so I came along. At the end
of the lesson on the first week I was there, she came up to
me to meet me. I was surprised, because she didn't do that
for the other newcomers.

Right away, she asked me to come home with her
for a meal. I was not used to this kind of hospitality! She
seemed to really want to spend time with me.

What ended up developing was a lot like a mother-
daughter relationship. She gave me spiritual mothering.
My own mother had not been able to do that for me, because she was not a believer, and she lived far away. My
spiritual mother and I talked a lot. We prayed together.
She gave me books to read. She began to teach me how
to pray with others (which I now teach to others), and we
ministered to others together. As I raised my children, she
became like a grandmother to them.

She conveyed rich blessings to me that I could not have

received from the particular pastors in the two churches to which I belonged during the course of our long relationship. When she died in her eighties, she bequeathed me her entire library of Christian books, so in a way she is still mentoring me.

—*J.E.*

It's Time to Change

Like Saul, we have to be taught who we really are. We have to be trained according to the vision of those God has placed over us. If this doesn't happen, we will be limited by our own capacity. Saul was thinking, *I'm just Kish's son. Nobody in my family has that kind of calling on their lives.*

But Samuel brings Saul into his private chambers for a meal. As spiritual children, we must be able to go to new levels in God, to the level of our spiritual parents. We must adapt our appetite and learn to digest the same meat as our spiritual parents do. The story tells us there were thirty other people at the table, and still more people feasting outside (1 Sam. 9:22). This is a picture of how there may be other people in your church or in the body of Christ to whom God has divinely connected you—but it is your leader who sees God's divine purpose in your life. He hands you the portion that has been prepared for you.

"And the cook lifted high the shoulder and what was on it [indicating that it was the priest's honored portion] and set it before Saul. [Samuel] said, See what was reserved for you" (v. 24). Apparently, when the Lord had revealed to Samuel the day before that Saul was coming, Samuel had told the cook, "God has revealed to me that I have a special guest coming. Set this portion apart. It will be reserved for him."

The things God had in store for Saul happened when he showed up. It's the same for you or me. If we are walking in divine obedience, we will not miss our divine connection. That's why when you come to the right church, you feel as if you have been there for years. It seems that you have known the pastor for a long time. After your first time there, you can say, "Wow, that was just what I needed." That's because the Holy Spirit knew you were coming. You can't reach your spiritual assignment before its time. The Father appointed the time when you should show up.

The next morning, Samuel spoke to Saul:

> They arose early and about dawn Samuel called Saul [who was sleeping] on the top of the house, saying, Get up, that I may send you on your way. Saul arose, and both he and Samuel went out on the street. And as they were going down to the outskirts of the city, Samuel said to Saul, Bid the servant pass on before us—and he passed on—but you stand still, first, that I may cause you to hear the word of God.
>
> —1 SAMUEL 9:26–27

No doubt you will need to let some people "pass on before you" also so that you can "stand still to hear the word of God." People that started out with you won't be the ones you end up with. This is your divine appointment, not theirs.

Many of us miss the mark here. We meet the right divine connection, we're in the right church, and we have the right pastor—but we don't wait on the word of God. We're not still enough so that the full word of the Lord concerning our lives can be imparted to us. So we "go" before our time instead of waiting on the timing of the Lord. We begin to operate by association and false authority.

> [We pray] that you may be invigorated and strengthened with all power according to the might of His glory … giving thanks to the Father, Who has qualified and made us fit to share the portion which is the inheritance of the saints (God's holy people) in the Light.
>
> —COLOSSIANS 1:11–12

Life-Changers

Read the following passages of Scripture. On the line following each scripture, write the name of the biblical character whose life was changed unexpectedly by God.

Acts 10 _____

Acts 16:11–15 _____

Acts 9:9–22 _____

1 Samuel 1 _____

Luke 19:1–10 _____

Which of these biblical characters can you identify with because of your own life circumstances? What is the connection? Write a few words about it.

1.   I can identify with _____ because

_____

_____

2.   How was this biblical character well positioned to hear God's life-changing message?

_____

_____

3.   How could he or she have "missed it"? Rewrite part of your chosen character's "script," adding some disobedience, missed guidance, and unresolved ending.

_____

_____

_____

_____

_____

Now, to build your faith, re-read your character's story.

True Riches Are in Your Father's House

We have to be careful that we're not forcing our spiritual fathers to give us our inheritance too early. We do this all the time. We want to look, act, and preach like our spiritual fathers before we know who we are called in the Spirit to be.

We're like the prodigal son, who lived in his father's house and who had an inheritance coming. But he forced it to be given to him early. He asked for his inheritance, but he hadn't matured enough to receive it. He had to lose his inheritance before he could become mature (through suffering and trials) and return to his father's house, profoundly repentant. Now he could understand the significance of being in his father's house. Now he could value being in his father's house more than anything else.

Like the prodigal son, we need to value being in our father's house more than anything we can do on our own. We need to wait for our spiritual father to take the initiative, while we are content to serve faithfully. And like Saul, we need to accept the word of God when it comes, even if we feel inadequate: "Then Samuel took the vial of oil and poured it on Saul's head and kissed him and said, Has not the Lord anointed you to be prince over His heritage Israel?" (1 Sam. 10:1).

The Essentials **You will come to your spiritual parents with a vision, a goal, and a desire; they are going to give you your spiritual destiny.**

Memory Verse We have not received the spirit of the world but the Spirit who is from God, that we may understand what God has freely given us.

—1 Corinthians 2:12, niv

To Your Father

Father, how will I recognize my earthly spiritual father or mother? Have I already missed him or her? How can I get on the right track? As I read about Saul and apply the story to my own life, here are some of the thoughts and fears and desires I became aware of:

_____

_____

_____

_____

I ask You to help me sort out what I'm thinking and feeling, Father. Please don't let me miss the next step in Your plan for me. Amen.

CHAPTER 4

The Anointing: Divine Order

*S*aul's story confirms that when you truly meet your divine connection, that person will have the anointing to help resolve your past while ushering you into the future.

When Saul encountered Samuel, Samuel did much more than tell him where to look for his father's donkeys. Samuel initiated the flow of spiritual inheritance into the life of Saul.

When you have left me today, you will meet two men by Rachel's tomb in the territory of Benjamin at Zelzah, and they will say to you, The donkeys you sought are found. And your father has quit caring about them and is anxious for you, asking, What shall I do about my son? Then you will go on from there and you will come to the oak of Tabor, and three men going up to God at Bethel will meet you there, one carrying three kids, another carrying three loaves of bread, and another carrying a skin bottle of wine. They will greet you and give you two loaves of bread, which you shall accept from their hand.

After that you will come to the hill of God, where the garrison of the Philistines is; and when you come to the city, you will meet a company of prophets coming down from the high place with harp, tambourine, flute, and lyre before them, prophesying. Then the Spirit of the Lord will come upon you mightily, and you will show yourself to be a prophet with them; and you will be turned into another man.

—1 Samuel 10:2–6

Three things happened for Saul: (1) His past assignment was brought to closure, (2) people were sent to sow into his life, and (3) he received divine direction about how to reach and operate on the next level.

Saul was transformed from a man chasing donkeys into a blessed prophet. His physical needs were met; a divine assignment was spoken over his life; he was anointed for that assignment. With one prophecy, one kiss, and one vial of oil, he was turned into a different man. The same prophetic gift that was upon Samuel instantly came upon Saul.

Samuel's ear had been trained to hear the Lord. He had been raised in the temple, weighed and birthed out in his prophetic anointing. When he met Saul years later, a man who had nothing prophetic in his background, Saul could become part of the divine company of prophets, too, because Samuel had already paid the price.

Samuel also connected Saul with a company of other prophets. Samuel was saying, in essence, "In order to walk in this assignment, you're going to have to change your company. You have to get among the kind of people that have the same kind of anointing." These new associations were not coming from some low place, but from a high place filled with music and prophesying. Your spiritual father will get you in a place where the Spirit of the Lord is moving all the time, with people who will have like spirits and the same anointing.

Can God Trust You?

Before you can be birthed out from your leader, he or she will look for two signs of readiness. Your leader will watch to see that you separate yourself from anything that is less than you are, and he or she will watch to see if you can follow instructions. After Samuel anointed and kissed Saul, he gave him several detailed instructions that Saul could not afford to miss.

The same pattern applies to us. Our leaders have to see us follow directions. We can't go where we want to go. This is the point at which many people miss God. They get a prophecy, "You're anointed of God. You're going to preach. I see you traveling all over the world." Then immediately their spiritual fathers say, "Let me pull back from that and teach you how to follow instructions." Instead of launching into their future, they need to settle the past and grow in their maturity. Samuel was saying to Saul, "You can't start being the prince of Israel yet."

The three men with the kids, the bread, and the wine were like a test. It was as if Samuel were saying to Saul, "Can I trust you with offerings? Can I trust you not to take advantage of this situation?" Samuel was mighty in the Lord and greatly feared. So he tested Saul, "Can I trust you not to use your association with me to get more than what I told you to take?"

Can your spiritual father trust you when he's not around? Can he trust you not to be manipulative? Can he trust you to take only what he told you to take—even though there are a host of things you could probably take—and see that you choose to uphold his word and follow instructions?

Samuel was testing Saul's character, to see if he could follow instructions and if he was balanced. He instructed Saul to receive only part of what the three men brought, because Saul wasn't ready for the whole amount. He had an assigned portion.

Getting Personal

I was one of those people whose character just was not mature enough to handle the call of God. He has been able to use me and bless me after all—eventually.

As a kid, I was a musical prodigy. Specifically, I could play the piano better than any of the teachers my parents could find for me. I played by ear, and I spurned instruction. By the time I was fourteen, I was accompanying the high school choir and playing the keyboard in church. I loved all the attention.

When people would say, "Oooh, you are so gifted!" I concluded that God was calling me to play the piano for Him. Nobody took me under their wing because I wouldn't let them. I thought I was better than all of them—at playing the piano, anyway. After I graduated from high school, I began to make connections with well-known Christian singers and to play for worship conferences. I put a lot of eggs into the one basket of my "call" to play the piano.

Things began to happen. My marriage was unhappy. I hurt my hand and couldn't play for a while. I had to take an "ordinary job" to help pay the bills. On top of that, I was asked to step down as the accompanist at my church. The reason was that someone had come along who was more talented! I was angry and hurt.

Eventually, after a very long time, I was desperate enough to submit to someone older and wiser in the Lord. I discovered that I had skipped a step—a very big one. I had not matured enough to carry this mantle because I had not submitted myself to anyone. And I had based everything on the cocky attitude that I was a great pianist and therefore I was special to God.

I decided to let God grow me up before I let myself touch the piano again. It was hard. What happened was that one of my daughters turned out to have the same talent I did, and as I found her a teacher and guided her through various decisions, I was able to do it with true (hard-won) wisdom.

Now she and I often play together, and I find as much satisfaction in one performance (done with a purified heart) than I did before in all of my activities. I do it for the glory of God and out of a grateful heart.

—M.C.

A good man leaves an inheritance [or moral stability and goodness] to his children's children, and the wealth of the sinner [finds its way eventually] into the hands of the righteous, for whom it was laid up.

—PROVERBS 13:22

Keep It to Yourself

Can your spiritual father trust you to keep your divine assignment to yourself until the time appointed?

When Saul got home, his uncle asked where he had been:

Saul's uncle said to him and to his servant, Where did you go? And Saul said, To look for the donkeys, and when we found them nowhere, we went to Samuel. Saul's uncle said, Tell me, what did Samuel say to you? And Saul said to his uncle, He told us plainly that the donkeys were found. *But of the matter of the kingdom of which Samuel spoke he told him nothing.*

—1 SAMUEL 10:14–16, EMPHASIS ADDED

Saul did not tell his uncle everything about his meeting with Samuel. Neither did Saul tell other people that he had been anointed. Later, Samuel (his spiritual father) did it: "And Samuel said to all the people, Do you see him whom the Lord has chosen, that none like him is among all the people? And all the people shouted and said, Long live the king!" (v. 24).

It is your leader's responsibility to make an announcement about you. You should never announce yourself. Not even Jesus, the Son of God and Word made flesh, announced Himself. John the Baptist announced Him. (See John 1.)

> In a multitude of words transgression is not lacking, but he who restrains his lips is prudent.
>
> —PROVERBS 10:19

Braggadocio

> Let another man praise you, and not your own mouth.
>
> —PROVERBS 27:2

In Genesis 37 read the story of how Joseph failed the bragging test.

1. What did Joseph brag about?

_____

2. What specific details most irked his brothers (and even his doting father)?

_____

_____

3. Was his bragging based on a true word from God?

_____

4. Was Joseph wise to talk this way to them?

_____

What would have been a wiser course of action?

_____

_____

5. Did God bring Joseph right away into the fulfillment of his word?

_____

Where did he have to go? (See Genesis 39–50.)

_____

How long did he live there? (See Genesis 50:26.)

_____

6. What did Joseph's bragging cost him?

_____

_____

_____

The kingdom of God often proves to be very paradoxical, full of seeming contradictions. If Joseph had been wiser, he would not have angered his brothers, and he would not have been sold into slavery. That would have meant that no one would have been in Egypt to save the lives of his family during the famine, and there would have been no Exodus, no Moses, perhaps no Israel—and Jesus would not have been born in Bethlehem. It could be said that God used Joseph's bragging to bring about His will.

7. Does this mean that we should go ahead and brag about God's anointing on us? Support your answer:

_____

_____

_____

_____

_____

8.   What is God's highest goal for us, which He will use even our mistakes to achieve?

_____

_____

9.   Did Joseph eventually achieve this high goal?

_____

10. In the end, was Joseph equipped to handle the fulfillment of God's word to him?

_____

11. Think about your own situation. Have you bragged about your calling? As you have moved into your calling, have you made some other "fatal error"? Can God redeem it? What might it cost you? Are you willing to pay the price to fulfill the will of God? Note your thoughts so you won't lose track of what you are learning:

_____

_____

_____

_____

The Test of Character

The "daughters of Zion" and the "sons of thunder" must be taught character. (See Isaiah 3:16–17; 4:4; Mark 3:17.) When the anointing is placed upon us, when the word of the Lord is spoken over our lives, when we have received our divine assignment, character must be worked in us through obedience.

Many people have great anointings and giftings, but they don't reach their divine destinies because they have refused counsel and instruction. They are running around without counsel, proclaiming themselves as someone who is anointed and calling their trials *spiritual warfare*. They don't know how to walk in obedience because they will not hear the counsel of their spiritual fathers and mothers.

Once we have received the mantle and anointing for a divine assignment, we must not be allowed to get away with anything. The Bible says, "A little leaven leaveneth the whole lump (Gal. 5:9, KJV). Before you know it, a little lying will lead to a lot of lying. A little cheating will lead to a lot of cheating, and a little stealing will lead to a whole lot of stealing.

We learn obedience through the things we suffer, and our suffering is sent to purify our character. The anointing alone doesn't establish our purposes. Our destiny cannot be established from just having a "high time" in church. It can't be established from goose bumps and tears. These things are only the beginning. Your divine purpose can be established only through counsel and obedience and growth in godly character.

The Essentials	To be able to walk in our divine inheritance, we must learn obedience and grow in godly character.
 Memory Verse	His divine power has given us everything we need for life and godliness through our knowledge of him who called us by his own glory and goodness. —2 PETER 1:3, NIV

To Your Father

My Father, I don't want to miss the way You have set before me. Please correct me if I have failed the test. Please enable me to receive the full portion of my inheritance. [Write your own prayer, based on your personal circumstances.]

_____

_____

_____

_____

I thank You for hearing my prayer, which I pray in the mighty name of Your Son, Jesus, amen.

CHAPTER 5

Stepping Over Authority

One of the major problems in the kingdom of God is not the failure to anoint people into *positions,* but instead the failure to train them how to stay in *grace.*

When God places an anointing upon you, the next step is to come under submission. The anointing in you must be channeled and guided. It must be placed under good counsel, because you are wearing something that you are unfamiliar with. You may feel pleased that the mightiness of God is resting upon you, but you haven't yet been trained to operate effectively in that particular anointing or gift.

This pattern applied even to the Son of God. The power in which Jesus walked required Him to stay under the constant tutelage of His Father. He kept asking when and how to use that power, what to say, what not to say, when to speak, and when not to speak. In His wilderness temptation, in the Garden of Gethsemane, and throughout His life on earth, Jesus could have spoken out and called upon the ministering angels to destroy the foul things that were coming up against Him, but He held His peace. Why? Because Jesus understood His anointing. He knew it was under subjection to the Father. And He couldn't step out from under that anointing at any time, or He would disconnect Himself from the Father and start following His own will.

Getting Personal

Many years ago, a prophet who visited our church called me out as a woman upon whom the "mantle of Elijah" would rest. His words affected me powerfully. I had always been involved in prayer and intercession, and I had been learning how to pray God's will for situations.

The visiting prophet left our church, and I started to press forward in my new calling. My pastor wanted me to start meeting with his wife to talk about what God was doing. But I had always found my pastor's wife to be difficult to talk with. She had some very strong opinions, and she seemed to always have the final word. So I kept finding excuses to avoid talking with her, while at the same time I began to gather with me a group of younger women to pray and intercede. This went on for years, and it seemed normal enough.

One year at Christmas, my pastor's wife went into a diabetic coma and never came out of it. After she died, her husband, who was getting up in years, decided to turn the church over to his nephew, an up-and-coming young man.

This created big changes for us. He shook things up. Among other things, he selected one of the members of my longtime prayer team to be on his staff, to be *hired* to lead part of the spiritual life of the church. I couldn't believe it. *I* was the one who had been chosen by God—or so I thought. I was, to say the least, bitter. I began to think I should move to another congregation where they might appreciate me better, but of course I felt I couldn't really start over anyplace.

One day, I heard a tape of Prophetess Bynum preaching about callings and obedience. I was so full of remorse!

I had not respected the guidance of my pastors, neither the first one nor the new one, and I had not allowed myself to be nurtured in the anointing I had been given. Now what should I do? I decided to do the only thing that brought me any peace: I would become a counselor for the young woman who was evidently shouldering my mantle. I would have to do it humbly, because I myself hadn't really learned my lessons very well, unless you count the ones I learned the hard way.

It's been all right. That was the right thing to do.

When Saul Stepped Over Authority

Saul came under Samuel's anointing, yet something that's all too common today happened to Saul after he was anointed. Saul stepped out of his anointing by stepping over Samuel's authority.

We pick up the story at the beginning of the thirteenth chapter of the Book of 1 Samuel, when Saul began his reign as king of Israel, leading Israel into battle at Gilgal. Samuel had told Saul to wait for him for seven days in Gilgal until the appointed time to offer sacrifice before going into battle. But when the seven days had passed and Samuel had not yet arrived, the people started to scatter. Saul was afraid, and he felt that he must do something *right then—with or without Samuel.* In an instant, he stepped out of obedience and into his human strength. His pride told him, "The people are leaving me. *I have to do something.*" Saul reacted to the people's actions and took that step out of authority: "So Saul said, Bring me the burnt offering and the peace offerings. And he offered the burnt offering [which he was forbidden to do]" (1 Sam. 13:9).

And just as he finished offering the burnt offering, behold, Samuel came! Saul went out to meet and greet him. Samuel said, What have you done? Saul said, Because I saw that the people were scattering from me, and that you did not come within the days appointed, and that the Philistines were assembled at Michmash, I thought, The Philistines will come down now upon me to Gilgal, and I have not made supplication to the Lord. So I forced myself to offer a burnt offering. And Samuel said to Saul, You have done foolishly! You have not kept the commandment of the Lord your God which He commanded you; for the Lord would have established your kingdom over Israel forever; but now your kingdom shall not continue; the Lord has sought out [David] a man after His own heart, and the Lord has commanded him to be prince and ruler over His people, because you have not kept what the Lord commanded you.

—1 SAMUEL 13:10–14

Had Saul obeyed the spiritual authority God had placed over his life, his kingdom would have been established forever. God's calling and gifts are irrevocable (Rom. 11:29). When you receive an impartation from your spiritual father, it is meant to last from generation to generation—because it comes from a spiritual lineage. It is your portion, your spiritual inheritance.

The deposit and transmission of this power is eternal because it originates from our heavenly Father. My life will end, but *the anointing never dies!* That's why I must walk according to the will of God and according to His precepts, so that when the time comes (and God begins to bring the people into my life that He has ordained to walk with me), I'll be able, through the laying on of hands, to impart that anointing to them. They in turn will lay hands on others at the appointed time and impart the same anointing. If the next generations are to be able to receive the divine impartation, the people who currently carry that impartation must walk strictly according to the will of God in every respect.

This spiritual principle was the focus of chapter two of this book. It runs like a golden cord throughout the entire book. When we are yielded to the will of others who are in spiritual leadership over us, then we are truly submitting to His authority.

Individuals, but Not Independent

In the following scriptures you will find examples of spiritual fathers/mothers and their sons/daughters. After each reference, first write the name of the father/mother, then the name of his or her son/daughter.

2 Timothy 1:5–6 _____

Mark 9:5–10 _____

Judges 11:34–37 _____

Philemon 10–13 _____

Ruth 2:2–3 _____

Matthew 3:17–4:10 _____

Esther 2–5 _____

1. Are all of these relationships identical with each other?

_____

List a few of the differences between them:

_____

_____

_____

2. Did these sons and daughters have to obey the same specific instructions?

_____

List a few of the different (even contradictory) directives that they were given:

_____

_____

_____

_____

Learning Submission

If you fail to submit to your spiritual fathers, then you will be shut off from the power of God. And when you are shut off from being successful under authority, you become a mere Bible teacher, not one whom God has called to impart truth into other people's lives. You can't impart what you don't have. You can't impart the Spirit of Truth when you are not willing to receive or walk according to this same Spirit.

It is only by the Spirit of Truth that we receive the authority and power of God. The same power and authority God gave to Jesus are now transmitted through the Holy Spirit to us, and the only way we can use it is to stay in obedience. We can't afford to "tap in and out" of obedience. We can't afford to do things our own way!

You must walk in obedience whether you agree or not. You are not submitting to a *person*; you are submitting to the *authority of God*. Submission is not about the person. It's not about whether we like something or not. Submission is about the incorruptible portion we hope to obtain from our heavenly Father.

Saul violated a spiritual principle when he offered the sacrifice on his own. He usurped the role of his spiritual father. When he violated and stepped over the authority of Samuel, he lost the anointing—yet he remained the king. But his kingdom didn't last forever. God removed the eternal blessing and gave his anointing to someone else. He was left to live out the season of his life that God had appointed without the prophetic anointing. Nothing could flow down into him anymore. Samuel had provided Saul's "flow," and as long as Saul stayed under Samuel, the prophetic anointing flowed down to him. When he stepped over it, it vanished. He was diminished to being merely a king of men.

Besides this, when Saul stepped over Samuel's authority, he came under the false anointing of Satan, the prince of the power of the air. Immediately he began to reap the fruits of a corrupt lineage.

Today, we have preachers, teachers, evangelists, and people sitting in the pews with anointings on their lives that are being diminished daily. When they stepped out of the will of God, they broke the divine pattern. Regardless of what the anointing was, because they stepped over the divine counsel over them, they can no longer carry the authority of their anointing. The Bible says we must submit one to another; submission keeps the anointing oil flowing down into your life.

Like Father, Like Son

Samuel told Saul that his disobedience had cost him his kingdom and that God had chosen a replacement king (David). Yet Saul regathered his army, in which his son Jonathan was a commander. We can learn valuable lessons from what happened next.

Read 1 Samuel 14:1–45.

1.   When Jonathan decided to take his armor-bearer and go over to the Philistine garrison, did he do it under obedience to his father, or did he act independently?

_____

_____

2.   Do we have any evidence that he had ever acted this way before?

_____

3.   From what you know of his story, did he continue to act this way? (See 1 Samuel 20:30–33.)

_____

4.   Was Jonathan punished by his father for doing what he did?

_____

5.   Look at 1 Samuel 14:28–33. Did Jonathan act in a spirit of *obedience* or in a spirit of *disobedience* to his father?

_____

6.   Did the troops act in a spirit of obedience to the Law of Moses (which forbids eating meat with the blood), or did they act in disobedience and defile themselves?

_____

7.   When Jonathan tasted honey (having missed hearing his father's strict command about fasting that day because he was away with his armor-bearer attacking the Philistines), why did he not suffer the consequences (death) that Saul had decreed for someone who should disobey? (See 1 Samuel 14:45.)

_____

8.   Do you agree or disagree with the argument that Jonathan should be spared?

_____

9.   Is your thinking influenced by (a) practical considerations and a desire to see Jonathan treated humanely, or (b) an appreciation

for the spiritual principle of submission?

_____

10. If Jonathan had *not* broken the ranks of submission, would obedience on his part have changed God's mind about his father, Saul? Why or why not?

_____

_____

11. Do you think that obedience on the part of Jonathan would have changed God's mind about Jonathan's own fate?

_____

(To find out Jonathan's fate, refer ahead to 1 Samuel 31:1–2. To help answer the question, see how God handled David's dishonesty in 1 Samuel 27:10–12 coupled with his reaction to distress in 1 Samuel 30:6–8.) Support your reasoning:

_____

_____

_____

12. Do you see the pattern of disobedience to authority?

_____

Trace it briefly through chapters 13 and 14 of 1 Samuel:

_____

_____

_____

_____

13. In your personal experience, have you seen a similar pattern in action?

_____

What is the one key to reversing the pattern? (See Isaiah 30:15; Jeremiah 15:19.)

_____

_____

Regardless of how high you go in ministry, no matter how high your calling and title may be, God requires you to be submitted and accountable. Even the president of the United States cannot function alone. He has to be accountable. He has to submit himself to others who are more knowledgeable than he is in specific areas.

Saul started out with thousands of men and ended up with six hundred. This is what happens when you begin to walk in disobedience and step over the authority God has given you. Instead of gaining, you lose. Your ministry begins to diminish, because only the authentic oil of the anointing causes multiplication. The oil of the anointing causes you to prosper. What the Lord allows to be spoken and poured into your life by your spiritual father is what causes your tent to expand.

> But when He, the Spirit of Truth (the Truth-giving Spirit) comes, He will guide you into all the Truth (the whole, full Truth). For He will not speak His own message [on His own authority]; but He will tell whatever He hears [from the Father; He will give the message that has been given to Him], and He will announce and declare to you the things that are to come [that will happen in the future].

He will honor and glorify Me, because He will take of (receive, draw upon) what is Mine and will reveal (declare, disclose, transmit) it to you. Everything that the Father has is Mine. That is what I meant when I said that He [the Spirit] will take the things that are Mine and will reveal (declare, disclose, transmit) it to you.

—JOHN 16:13–15

Saul's Third Encounter With Authority

God sent Samuel back to Saul again. He told Saul to go to battle with Amalek. Very specifically, Samuel told Saul, "Utterly destroy all they have; do not spare them, but kill both man and woman, infant and suckling, ox and sheep, camel and donkey" (1 Sam. 15:3). Saul began to do what the Lord had commanded. He assembled the men and went forth to Amalek. There was a great battle. But once again, Saul failed to do *all* that God had instructed him to do. He spared Agag, the king of Amalek, and the best of the livestock.

I can just hear God say, "Here we go again." All means *all*. Once again, Saul had disobeyed. When Samuel found out, he "was grieved and angry [with Saul], and he cried to the Lord all night" (v. 11).

Any real spiritual father or mother would weep and cry when the anointing is lifted off of someone, because it's as if that person had died. There's nothing worse than having the anointing lifted off your life because of disobedience—especially when you've received a rich impartation of an untainted anointing.

It's a tragedy. Samuel had faithfully transmitted his anointing to Saul, but Saul disobeyed him three times in a row. (For his part, Samuel continued to walk out the word he had been given. He kept himself clean before the Father, and God kept him separated and consecrated.)

From Samuel, Saul had received a pure impartation and good instruction. But he was willful, and he tainted it. What's worse, he tried to blame the people for his bad decision. (See 1 Samuel 15:14–15.) But we know that the people only did what they did because Saul had broken the orderly flow of the anointing. They spared the best of the sheep and oxen because Saul had spared King Agag. Always look for the pattern. Whenever there is disobedience in the leadership, it breeds disobedience in the people.

Samuel tried to remind Saul of how God had raised him into his position and of the responsibilities that came with kingship (vv. 17–19). Saul's response is interesting. He contradicted Samuel's interpretation of events, and he ended by saying that the sheep and oxen had been preserved for a good reason, to be sacrificed "to the Lord *your* God" (v. 21, emphasis added).

If you have been called under the hand of the Lord into leadership, you need to keep yourself in check. You need to let your mind go back to where God brought you from, to who and what you were before the Father sent this great impartation of His power to you. And you need to operate in the fear of the Lord. Saul had not cultivated a relationship with God. He considered Samuel to be his intermediary to God—yet he persisted in acting the opposite to Samuel's counsel. When you step over an anointing, it becomes perversion. Once the spirit of perversion has entered in, it presents a distorted reflection of the truth of God, and it actually yields the opposite result: it reverses His commands.

You see, the enemy wants to make us believe that the Lord is more interested in what we sacrifice to Him than He is in our obedience. "Samuel said, Has the Lord as great a delight in burnt offerings and sacrifices as in obeying the voice of the Lord? Behold, to obey is better than sacrifice, and to hearken than the fat of rams" (1 Sam. 15:22).

Be careful when you begin to operate in and transmit God's power. His power within you must be properly submitted under spiritual authority. Unbridled power can corrupt the anointing God has imparted and can make it impossible for you to transmit it to others.

The Essentials

To reach the end of our lives without losing God's anointing, we must walk in complete obedience to God and to our spiritual leaders.

Memory Verse

To obey is better than sacrifice, and to heed is better than the fat of rams. For rebellion is like the sin of divination, and arrogance like the evil of idolatry.

—1 SAMUEL 15:22–23, NIV

To Your Father

My Father, I pray in the words of Psalm 61:1–5 [NIV], which were written by David, who received Saul's anointing after Saul failed. I too, like the psalmist, want to stay in the shelter of Your wings:

Hear my cry, O God;
     listen to my prayer.
From the ends of the earth I call to you,
     I call as my heart grows faint;
     lead me to the rock that is higher than I.
For you have been my refuge,
     a strong tower against the foe.
I long to dwell in your tent forever
     and take refuge in the shelter of your wings.
For you have heard my vows, O God;
     you have given me the heritage of those who fear your name.

[You can find a continuation of this prayer in verses 6–8 of Psalm 61, and in Psalm 62.]

Humbly I say amen.

The Generational Curse

*A*s we saw in Saul's life, disobedience runs from generation to generation. Another Old Testament family whose pattern we can trace is the family of kings: Amaziah, Uzziah, Jotham, Ahaz, and Hezekiah.

Generation to Generation

Amaziah

"Amaziah ... did right in the Lord's sight, but not with a perfect or blameless heart" (2 Chron. 25:1–2). He kept the Law of Moses, but he failed to listen to the counsel of God through the prophet in his own house.

> So the anger of the Lord was kindled against Amaziah, and He sent to him a prophet, who said, Why have you sought after the gods of the people, which could not deliver their own people out of your hand? As he was talking, the king said to him, Have we made you the king's counselor? Stop it! ... The prophet stopped but said, I know that God has determined to destroy you, because you have done this and ignored my counsel.
>
> —2 CHRONICLES 25:15–16

When pride is in operation, a spirit of control causes leaders to act with false authority. They start manipulating people to do things that aren't the will of the Father. The spirit of control quenches the anointing in the people that would otherwise strengthen the leaders' ministry. But if these people stay steadfast to God, He will ultimately bring judgment upon the false leadership, while moving the people out of harm's way.

So if you're a leader, when you see issues running like a cord throughout your church—attitudes, dispositions, character issues, and so on—you need to check your own character. You need to check what you are birthing and imparting into your people, because they are only giving back what they have received from your hands.

Amaziah was mighty, and his kingdom was strengthened until he became exalted in his own eyes. When he felt that he no longer needed to seek after God or to receive the word of the Lord, Amaziah's sins ultimately led to death.

Uzziah

Uzziah watched his father, and he saw what had happened in the kingdom.

> Uzziah…did right in the Lord's sight, to the extent of all that his father Amaziah had done. He set himself to seek God in the days of Zechariah, who instructed him in the things of God; and as long as he sought (inquired of, yearned for) the Lord, God made him prosper.
>
> —2 CHRONICLES 26:3–5

Uzziah submitted himself to the tutelage of Zechariah, and, as a result, he became strong in the Lord. The list of his accomplishments is long. (See 2 Chronicles 26:6–15.)

However, his father's disobedience had been planted deep in Uzziah's soul, and he eventually repeated the pattern. "But when [King Uzziah] was strong, he became proud to his destruction; and he trespassed against the Lord his God, for he went into the temple of the Lord to burn incense on the altar of incense" (v. 16).

At the beginning of his reign, King Uzziah was under spiritual authority. But then he became great in his own eyes and stepped over it, usurping an authority that was not his. He wasn't supposed to be a priest; he was meant to be a king only.

Once again, as we saw in the story of Saul, strength bred pride, which led to disobedience. We must be careful when we start seeing the fruits of our labor and when our ministry gains recognition, because pride can creep in and create a foothold for this foul spirit.

When Uzziah trespassed against the Lord by going into the tabernacle to burn incense, Azariah the priest went in after him along with eighty priests of the Lord—men of courage, discipline, and rebuke.

> They opposed King Uzziah and said to him, It is not for you, Uzziah, to burn incense to the Lord, but for the priests, the sons of Aaron, who are set apart to burn incense. Withdraw from the sanctuary; you have trespassed, and that will not be to your credit and honor before the Lord God. Then Uzziah was enraged.
>
> —2 Chronicles 26:18–19

When people become prideful and strong in their own eyes, they become enraged any time they are corrected. Uzziah's anger led to further disobedience:

> And while he was enraged with the priests, leprosy broke out on his forehead before the priests in the house of the Lord, beside the incense altar. And as Azariah the chief priest and all the priests looked upon him, behold, he was leprous on his forehead! So they forced him out of there; and he also made haste to get out, because the Lord had smitten him. And King Uzziah was leper to the day of his death, and, being a leper, he dwelt in a separate house, for

he was excluded from the Lord's house. And Jotham his son took charge of the king's household, ruling the people of the land.

—2 Chronicles 26:19–21

When Uzziah stepped over the spiritual authority God had appointed for him, he became a diseased king under a false anointing. The same thing is happening in the church today. Some leaders who have stepped out of their appointed authority are still preachers or evangelists, but they're diseased. They have stepped out of the will of the Lord by way of their own strength.

Evidence of God's Anointing

Read 2 Corinthians 12:7–10.

1. Was Paul's "thorn in the flesh" sent from God or from Satan (v. 7)?

_____

2. Why did he have this problem (v. 7)?

_____

3. Why did God not heal the problem (v. 9)?

_____

4. Why was Paul glad about his chronic problem (v. 10)?

_____

5. Was it only this particular "thorn" for which he was grateful?

_____

_____

List the types of problems that he included in "welcome weaknesses" (v. 10).

_____

_____

_____

6.   Explain how a chronic _physical, mental, emotional,_ or _relational_ problem can help us walk in our anointing.

_____

_____

_____

7.   Explain how a chronic _spiritual_ problem cause us to step out of our anointing.

_____

_____

_____

Jotham

In 2 Chronicles 27, we meet Uzziah's son Jotham, who was a man of God. "Jotham grew mighty, for he ordered his ways in the sight of the Lord his God" (2 Chron. 27:6).

Jotham broke the pattern of his forefathers. He was the third generation, which represents the number of divine completion. Jotham had most likely heard about what happened to his grandfather and also watched his father, Uzziah. He started ruling when his father became leprous, so he guarded what he did and walked in a level of obedience to God.

But the generational pattern still had an effect on his reign, because "he did right in the sight of the Lord, *to the extent of all that his father Uzziah had done*" (v. 2, emphasis added). He did not surpass their level of obedience.

> If you are willing and obedient, you shall eat the good of the land; but if you refuse and rebel, you will be devoured by the sword. For the mouth of the Lord has spoken it.
> —ISAIAH 1:19–20

Ahaz

The pattern of iniquity picked up again in the following generation:

> Ahaz...did not do right in the sight of the Lord....But he walked in the ways of the kings of Israel and even made molten images for the Baals. And he burned incense in the Valley of Ben-hinnom [son of Hinnom] and burned his sons as an offering, after the abominable customs of the [heathen] nations whom the Lord drove out before the Israelites.
> —2 CHRONICLES 28:1–3

Ahaz, Jotham's son, became twice as corrupt as his forefathers—burning incense to false gods and even sacrificing his own sons, to whom he was supposed to hand his mantle. Leaders with false anointings will destroy the people under their rule instead of birthing them out.

History repeated itself in the demise of Ahaz. Four generations after his great-grandfather Amaziah had defeated the Edomites—but had brought back their gods to worship—the Edomites defeated King Ahaz. Disobedience and false authority keep getting worse from generation to generation, with each generation becoming more wicked.

Getting Personal

I have chronic asthma, from which I have sought healing for years. I've been healed of other things, but never the asthma. It was getting me down.

At my church, I have been part of the "spiritual clean-up crew" for five or six years. (That's supposed to be a humorous way of describing the intercessors, the group of people who pray for the church.) I have a close relationship with everyone on the team, especially the leader, and sometimes I lead our little prayer meeting in her absence. As you might expect, this type of an assignment involves some spiritual warfare.

One day recently, I started to think about *humility* as a kind of camouflage outfit to keep the enemy forces from seeing me. Instead of showing off all my flashy spiritual armory, I decided to hide behind the things like my asthma, which definitely keeps me humble and weak. I realized that my work problems keep me humble too, because I have to keep asking God for patience and wisdom to cope with my boss. So that was the first lesson: difficulties keep me humble, and humility keeps me "out of sight" from enemy forces.

Then I realized that both problems are purifying my character more and more. They drive me to God, and they keep me from relying on myself. I am beginning to be grateful for both the asthma *and* a bad boss! (Now, God can feel free to heal me and deliver me any time He wants, but I'm glad to be getting some mileage out of these problems.)

—K.S.

Hezekiah

Finally, Hezekiah was set into power with grace. He was the fifth generation after Amaziah (five represents grace). Hezekiah fully recognized that his forefathers had gravely disobeyed God; he could clearly see the penalties they had paid.

He set himself both to seek the Lord and to restore the temple. He started by putting the things of God back into divine order. Hezekiah opened the doors of the temple (which are symbolic of the heart) and repaired them. Then he made a declaration that exposed the work of the enemy, and he had the priests confess the sins of the fathers that had led to their captivity. Finally, he started the orderly flow of the anointing by declaring a new covenant with God. (See 2 Chronicles 29:3–15.) Through Hezekiah, the cord of disobedience was broken, and the people were restored to order and prosperity.

Restoring the Anointing

To recover an anointing, you must go back to where you lost it. This involves both repentance and a resumption of covenant responsibilities. Read 2 Chronicles 29 to review what Hezekiah did to recover the anointing that his fathers had lost.

1.   Do you feel you may have lost an anointing, and/or do you feel that someone close to you has?

_____

What is the evidence that it has been lost, and when/how was it lost?

_____

_____

_____

_____

2. Hezekiah's opening and repairing of the temple doors corresponds to the first step of recovering any anointing: opening and repairing our hearts, which have fallen into disrepair and disuse. (Our bodies are temples of the Holy Spirit, and our hearts are doors through which God comes in.) Another word for this is *repentance,* or turning again. How—in specific ways—can you open and repair your heart?

_____

_____

_____

3. Many people stop after this step, because it *is* a major step to recognize that repentance is needed. But is opening and repairing our hearts enough to recover the anointing that has been lost? (Was it enough for Hezekiah?)

_____

4. Is recovering an anointing an individual act, or does it involve other people? Why?

_____

_____

_____

5. Whom did Hezekiah involve besides himself? (See verses 5, 20, 28–29.)

_____

_____

_____

_____

6. In the personal situation you reviewed above, who else will need to become involved in recovering the anointing?

_____

_____

Whether you are part of the first or fifth spiritual generation, whether you are a spiritual father or mother, or a son or daughter, the spirit of disobedience can be broken! You can find and stay in your place in God, no matter what you've been through in the past, because Jesus has gone before you. Turn your face to seek the Lord, and walk after the Spirit, praying acceptably to God the Father. He will help you set your spiritual house in order so that you can receive a heavenly blessing.

In the same way, every believer should walk in purification, even if you don't function in a spiritual office. For example, you might be thinking, _I'm not a pastor, so this doesn't apply to me._ I beg to differ. Every member in every church has a following, whether you are a staff member who practically lives at church or you attend church only once a week. If you are active in the church, somebody is drawn to the flow of the anointing upon you. Your lifestyle causes others either to see God and embrace the divine flow of the anointing—or to be hurt by disobedience.

God is crying out for sanctification and purification, both for our sakes and so the orderly flow of the anointing can flow without hindrance down to the next generations. "For the Lord God…bestows [presents] grace and favor and [future] glory (honor, splendor, and heavenly bliss)! No good thing will He withhold from those who walk uprightly" (Ps. 84:11).

In this hour, we cannot afford to be self-willed. We cannot afford to insist upon our own way, because if we do, everything the Lord has lined up in our lives will be transferred to somebody else. Hear me. Your life and your anointing do not belong to you alone. You are accountable to the authority of God through the spiritual fathers that have gone before you. And remember, no matter what may have happened in the past, you will be blessed if you are obedient. You don't have to stay under a curse!

> Do you not believe that I am in the Father, and that the Father is in Me? What I am telling you I do not say on My own authority and of My own accord; but the Father Who lives continually in Me does the (His) works (His own miracles, deeds of power).... I assure you, most solemnly I tell you, if anyone steadfastly believes in Me, he will himself be able to do the things that I do.... [I Myself will grant] whatever you ask in My Name [as presenting all that I AM], so that the Father may be glorified and extolled in (through) the Son.
>
> —JOHN 14:10, 12–13

Elisha's Double Portion

Elisha gives us a positive example of the anointing and mantle of a spiritual father (Elijah) being passed down to his spiritual son (Elisha). Elijah walked with God, and Elisha learned from him by walking with him daily for years. When Elijah was about to be taken into heaven, Elisha positioned himself to receive a double portion of his anointing. (See 2 Kings 2:9–21.)

God will come into the midst of whatever you're doing and send you a spiritual father to impart a new anointing upon your life. When he comes, your spirit must be willing to drop what you're doing and follow after that mantle, no matter how great your "field" is.

Elijah was a man of integrity, a fearless reformer who was mighty in prayer. Elisha received a double portion of Elijah's anointing. With us as with him, this indicates that the portion that flows to you from someone else's measure meets the portion already within you. As you walk steadily in your double portion, even more anointing is placed upon you because of your obedience. A godly anointing *multiplies*.

The Essentials

You will be able to impart your anointing to spiritual sons or daughters, if you carry with righteousness the anointing you have received from your spiritual fathers.

Memory Verse

Trust in the LORD with all your heart and lean not on your own understanding; in all your ways acknowledge him, and he will make your paths straight. Do not be wise in your own eyes; fear the LORD and shun evil. This will bring health to your body and nourishment to your bones.

—PROVERBS 3:5–8, NIV

To Your Father

Father in heaven, I ask you to bless _____, my spiritual father [or mother] on earth. I ask you to help _____ to be steadfast in every way.

I also ask you to help me to carry the mantle I have been given. I want to walk in holy fear of You. [Write a continuation of this prayer to fit your own circumstances.]

_____

_____

_____

_____

_____

In the name of Jesus, amen.

CHAPTER 7

The Power of Rebuke

*C*orrection from your spiritual father will keep you under spiritual authority and keep you from trusting in your own strength, thereby missing all that God has destined for you. If you're able to receive correction in your spirit, then you can receive God's wisdom. He helps, saves, and has mercy on everyone. But He *trains* and *corrects* the wise.

> The ear that listens to the reproof [that leads to or gives] life will remain among the wise. He who refuses and ignores instruction and correction despises himself, but he who heeds reproof gets understanding. The reverent and worshipful fear of the Lord brings instruction in Wisdom, and humility comes before honor.
>
> —PROVERBS 15:31–33

A Loving Father Corrects His Children

When God puts you in the position to be rebuked, whether it's for something you've said, done, felt, or believed, He's announcing to you that He loves you. Many times we doubt God's love for us. We expect Him to show us His love the way a human being would—because we don't have a true concept of His divine nature. But God doesn't express His love to us through gifts, houses, cars, or goose bumps. He confirms His love when He corrects and rebukes us. In His Word, we read:

> Those whom I [dearly and tenderly] love, I tell their faults
> and convict and convince and reprove and chasten [I
> discipline and instruct them]. So be enthusiastic and in
> earnest and burning with zeal and repent [changing your
> mind and attitude].
>
> —REVELATION 3:19

If you are "enthusiastic" when rebuke comes your way, it shows
you're excited to get it right. You'll be thinking, *OK, where did I miss
it? I'm being corrected because I know that God has a destiny for me.*
If God is correcting your life, He has a portion for you, and He's
getting your spirit ready for it.

If you remain open to correction, you will impart life to others.
But if you don't remain open to correction, you will impart the spirit
of error. Imparting the spirit of error happens too easily—usually
without either party even realizing it. This is what happened with
King Saul and Jonathan. If you are in the position of a leader, you
are communicating to others (even without words). Your life is
saying, "See the way I'm going? Follow me." Most people don't read
their Bibles; they read your life. Don't impart to them anything
you do incorrectly because of rejecting God's correction.

> He who heeds instruction and correction is [not only him-
> self] in the way of life [but also] is a way of life for others.
> And he who neglects or refuses reproof [not only himself]
> goes astray [but also] causes to err and is a path toward
> ruin for others.
>
> —PROVERBS 10:17

Character of the One Who Rebukes

**How do you know if you should listen to the person who corrects
you? How do you know if that person is imparting God's good**

character to you? To be sure of what you're looking for, read what Paul wrote to his spiritual son Titus in Titus 1:6–2:8, and answer the questions.

1.   Many *desirable* character traits are listed in these verses. Write down as many of them as you can find:

_____

_____

_____

_____

2.   Which of these traits is easiest for you to overlook in someone? Why is that?

_____

_____

_____

3.   What *undesirable* character traits of "unruly" and "rebellious" people are listed in Titus 1:10–16?

_____

_____

_____

4.   What does Paul want Titus to do about those people?

_____

5.   Should you accept corrections and rebukes from such people?

_____

6.   Since no one has a *perfect* character, does this mean that we are "off the hook" regarding accepting correction from our leaders?

_____

Hebrews 13:17 tells us what attitude to have toward the instructions of our spiritual leaders. What simple reason does it give for accepting corrections from them?

_____

7.   If you can think of a time when you were rebuked or corrected (not necessarily singled out; perhaps you sat in the congregation and heard a strong sermon), think about how the lessons you have just learned might apply. Is there anything you would change about your reactions? Did you receive the correction and notice good results? Record your thoughts.

_____

_____

_____

The apostle Paul spoke these words to Titus:

> Paul, a bondservant of God and an apostle (a special messenger) of Jesus Christ (the Messiah) to stimulate and promote the faith of God's chosen ones and to lead them on to accurate discernment and recognition of and acquaintance with the Truth which belongs to and harmonizes with and tends to godliness.
>
> —TITUS 1:1

Paul was saying, "I'm a servant who has been ordained by God. I'm writing this letter to you, Titus, because I'm about to say some strong things. I'm going to correct you. I'm concerned with 'cutting out' character in you."

So many believers today get too anxious, asserting, "Oh, the Lord gave me a word; He gave me a word." If He gave you a word, it will keep. In the meantime, your spiritual leaders need to carve character in you to bring you to the level where you can handle the word you received.

Why must you become submissive to the power of correction? Because it teaches your spirit how to renounce all ungodliness. How can you renounce ungodliness if you don't know what it is? Our heavenly Father has to rebuke us (through His Word and our leaders) to expose ungodliness so that the next time it comes around, we can recognize it and renounce it.

There's so much "mixture" in the body of Christ that it's hard for people to understand what is holy and what isn't, what constitutes sin and what doesn't. If your spiritual father corrects you, you don't have to go around saying, "Well, I don't know if that's wrong or not, but I don't feel convicted about it, so it doesn't bother me."

Challenging Rebuke

Cain brought the fruit of the ground as an offering to God. His brother Abel came and offered a lamb. (See Genesis 4:1–6.) The Father was pleased with Abel's offering, which made Cain upset. God had to rebuke him.

God told Cain, "If you do well, will you not be accepted? And if you do not do well, sin crouches at your door; its desire is for you, but you must master it" (Gen. 4:7).

God wasn't concerned with Cain's feelings; He was more concerned with keeping sin from "crouching at the door" of his life. Anybody can make a mistake. But when the person rejects correction, the mistake becomes sin.

Sometimes we start to believe that we are beyond correction. I see it all the time: "I know the Lord. I can discern the way myself." But when you reject correction, the first thing that happens is that a spirit of deception comes into the situation. Then you start doing things with the wrong motive, as Cain did: "And Cain said to his brother, Let us go out to the field. And when they were in the field, Cain rose up against Abel his brother and killed him" (v. 8).

What happens next? *Murder.* It can be murder with your mouth—killing ideas in the church, killing people's spirits in the church, killing spiritual authority, killing your marriage and your children's self-esteem. When you walk in rebellion against a rebuke, you begin to attack everything around you, especially the things of God.

When you get a bad attitude after being corrected, it's more than just anger—your spirit has rejected the Lord. And when you reject God in any way, the spirit of deception starts perverting everything that comes from the pulpit. It is vitally important to recognize this. If you don't, you become vulnerable to the devil's strategies, and, before you know it, you are sitting smack dab in the middle of the enemy's camp.

When God confronted Cain about what he had done to Abel, Cain responded, "Am I my brother's keeper?" (v. 9). Disrespectful! Cain was talking to *God!* He had rejected the rebuke, and his sin multiplied. Now he was in a state of full-blown rebellion.

Obey your spiritual leaders and submit to them [continually recognizing their authority over you], for they are constantly keeping watch over your souls and guarding your spiritual welfare, as men who will have to render an account [of their trust]. [Do your part to] let them do this with gladness and not with sighing and groaning, for that would not be profitable to you [either].

—Hebrews 13:17

Getting Personal

I was a self-starter, a man on a mission to succeed in life. I felt that God wanted me to devote my attention to getting a good education, which I did, and then I was supposed to become successful in business. Nobody told me how important it was to grow in having a mature and godly character. I derived my information about successful living from the world around me, and I prided myself on my common sense and ambition.

My pastor told me later that he could see a pattern in my life, and he didn't think it would lead to any kind of success ultimately. It was a kind of cockiness. Basically, I acted like the biggest kid on the playground. One day, because I had just walked all over another guy in the church, Pastor O. spoke to me about it.

My first reaction was anger; I could just feel the blood boiling in my spirit. But something about the way Pastor O. stood there made me pause. It reminded me of the way my grandma used to stand sometimes. He said these words: "Do you want to be a man of God, or do you want to be a man of the world?"

He was rebuking me! I was disoriented. Then I just broke.

In one moment, I realized that I'd been running from God for a long time. I had to practically drag myself up off the floor to say, "Pastor, forgive me. Please show me how to be a man of God."

I never had a godly model of manhood, so I had taken what the world had to offer. Now my pastor was catching up with me—which meant God was—and I could see that I'd better cooperate with a process, or wander around forever looking for something that would feel good.

It's been painful sometimes. But I would have to say it's worth it. I am a better man and a better husband, and my baby son has a better father. I have booted the Big "I" off the throne, and I'm trusting that the Big "I AM" will keep teaching me how to be remade in His image!

—J. J.

Rebellion Is Witchcraft

The Bible says that rebellion is as the sin of witchcraft (1 Sam. 15:23). When you reject correction, the spirit of witchcraft will try to take over. You will have put a hex on yourself. A spirit of rebellion can tear your life apart.

"And [the Lord] said, What have you done? The voice of your brother's blood is crying to Me from the ground" (Gen. 4:10). Whenever God's creation is being abused or hindered from fulfilling the purpose for which He created it, the offense against it comes up before God. He will bring it to your attention, usually through another person.

To avoid the divine "domino effect," you'd better say "Yes, Lord," when He comes to you about something small. If you reject Him, the curse of being driven away from God's presence altogether will take effect—and that means losing your spiritual inheritance.

The Father will say, "If I can't get you to submit to the pastor, and I can't get you to submit to correction, then I can't take you any further."

"Correct, Rebuke, and Encourage"

The Bible is full of exhortations about rebuke. Using a concordance, look up the word *rebuke*, and locate a few scriptures that instruct us as to how or why to receive (or give) rebuke. If you don't have

a concordance, you could start by looking up the following references: Proverbs 27:5; Ecclesiastes 7:5; Luke 17:3; 2 Timothy 4:2.

1.   Write out one of the scriptures you looked up. Choose one that speaks to you in a particular way.

_____

_____

_____

2.   God wants us to walk on a straight road to heaven. Read Jeremiah 2:19. If another human being doesn't rebuke us for our misbehavior, what else will rebuke us?

_____

God's process is to correct, train, and bless you now so that when you come into divine purpose, you are ready. If you stay submitted to spiritual authority, you can rise to a level where you are walking in the blessings of God because you understand His principles. You won't offend God, because you hear His voice and obey. Are you ready to experience the fullness of His divine presence? Then let Him try your spirit through submission. Embrace the power of rebuke.

The Essentials

Accept godly correction from your spiritual father. It will keep you from trusting in your own strength, and you won't lose your spiritual inheritance.

Memory Verse

Blessed is the man whom God corrects;
so do not despise the discipline of
the Almighty.
For he wounds, but he also binds up;
he injures, but his hands also heal.

—JOB 5:17–18, NIV

To Your Father

Father God, I know I have rejected Your correction. I ask You to break the spirit of rebellion out of me and make me a servant. Create in me a clean heart. Renew a right spirit within me. [Continue this prayer in your own words.]

_____

_____

_____

_____

Thank You for patiently correcting me and for sending Your Son, Jesus, through whom I can walk freely in obedience, and in whose name I pray. Amen.

CHAPTER 8

The Absence of Correction

*G*od will make sure that you don't outrun, mishandle, or abuse the spiritual greatness He has put within you. The Scriptures show us that God disciplines and prepares us to receive our inheritance.

Purposes and Plans Are Established by Counsel

Proverbs 20:18 instructs us, "Purposes and plans are established by counsel." The Father reveals His plans and purposes through the process of wise counsel. He will never give you an assignment that doesn't require counsel. Your personal plans may be accomplished without asking anybody any questions, but a good sign of a plan from the Lord is that *you'll need some help with it.*

Learn to pull back when people start giving you compliments: "Oh, you're anointed.... God's going to use you." They don't realize how easy they are making it for you to forget that an anointing comes with rules and stipulations about where you can go, whom you can be with, and what you can do.

Wise Counsel

Read Psalm 73:21–26.

1.   The psalmist is honest about his ability to seek God. What

kind of a difficulty had he just been through (vv. 21–22)?

_____

_____

2.   Had he been in a rational state of mind?

_____

3.   Had he been able to make good judgments during that time?

_____

4.   How does he reveal that he does not rely on his own strength—even to seek God (vv. 23–24)?

_____

_____

5.   Whose strength does he rely on?

_____

6.   Who takes the initiative to improve the situation, God or the psalmist?

_____

7.   What rewards is the psalmist looking forward to (vv. 24, 26)?

_____

_____

When I get through being used by God, I don't want to find myself anointed but shipwrecked. People who are not under submission to the proper authority get confronted with demons that have been designed to match their strength. That's what happened to Samson:

And the Israelites again did what was evil in the sight of the Lord, and the Lord gave them into the hands of the Philistines for forty years. And there was a certain man of Zorah, of the tribe of the Danites, whose name was Manoah; and his wife was barren and had no children. And the Angel of the Lord appeared to the woman and said to her, Behold, you are barren and have no children, but you shall become pregnant and bear a son. Therefore beware and drink no wine or strong drink and eat nothing unclean. For behold, you shall become pregnant and bear a son. No razor shall come upon his head, for the child shall be a Nazirite to God from birth, and he shall begin to deliver Israel out of the hands of the Philistines.

—JUDGES 13:1–5

Samson was a *Nazirite*, which means God had set him apart. He couldn't run around with just anybody. The Philistines were the enemies of God and His people, so Samson was raised up to become one of the judges (defenders) for the nation. Samson wasn't blessed with the spiritual inheritance simply because God liked his mamma. There was a divine purpose for his strength.

But we'll never know what his full destiny would have looked like, because as soon as he grew up, Samson began to mess it up. First, he saw a Philistine girl in Timnah, and he said to his parents, "I like that girl; get her for me." They didn't approve, but they went to see her with him:

Then Samson and his father and mother went down to Timnah and came to the vineyards of Timnah. And behold, a young lion roared against him. And the Spirit of the Lord came mightily upon him, and he tore the lion as he would have torn a kid, and he had nothing in his hand; *but he did not tell his father or mother what he had done.*

—JUDGES 14:5–6, EMPHASIS ADDED

As I read these verses, God kept bringing to my attention the fact that Samson didn't tell his parents about killing the lion. Then God whispered in my spirit, "Had Samson told his parents that he'd killed a lion, it would have given them an opportunity to say, 'Don't misuse the strength that God has given you. It's not for your own purposes.'"

Instead, Samson continued to Timnah, where he had a conversation with the Philistine woman he wanted to marry. Then he began the journey home by the same way. In passing the carcass of the lion, he found that a swarm of bees had made honey in it.

Remember, Samson wasn't supposed to touch or eat anything unclean. But he wanted it, so he ate the honey anyway, right out of the dead animal, even though his parents had raised him not to touch anything unclean. He had started to recognize the power of God on his life. I can just imagine him thinking, *I killed the lion with my bare hands. I can do whatever I want.*

Believers do the same thing today. They start to think, *I'm mature. I don't have to go to church for every service. I don't have to come on time. I don't have to do what they say; that's for the others who are still babies.* Wrong!

Wisdom

The Book of Proverbs is a collection of advice for life. Read the first seven introductory verses of the first chapter.

1. Did the counsel contained in the Book of Proverbs come through human means?

_____

2. Which verse showed you the answer?

_____

3. Into these few verses are packed many reasons to listen to wise counsel. List at least six of these:

_____

_____

_____

_____

_____

_____

4. What is the name for someone who rejects wisdom and discipline (v. 7)?

_____

5. What is the origin of all wisdom (v. 7)?

_____

> Where there is no counsel, purposes are frustrated, but with many counselors they are accomplished.
>
> —Proverbs 15:22

The Age of Accountability

Not only did Samson eat the unclean honey, but also he gave some to his parents. He defiled them. After that, they stopped challenging him. This can happen to us, too, so spiritual parents need to stay on their guard in the Spirit.

Then a whole series of events happened. Samson gave a riddle, and his bride coaxed the meaning out of him (Judg. 14:13–18). He was so furious about it that "the Spirit of the Lord came upon" him, and he killed thirty men and took their garments for spoil (v. 19).

(The Spirit of the Lord came upon Samson every time the Philistines did something to him, because they were God's enemies. However, that didn't guarantee that Samson was killing with the right motive. God can use us even when we're wrong, in spite of our weakness. But if we're not careful, we'll be working for the kingdom while on our way to hell. Just because you have the power of God on your life does not mean that you are totally submitted to the will of God. You may get the victory, but it doesn't prove you were right.)

> My son, hear the instruction of your father; reject not nor forsake the teaching of your mother. For they are a [victor's] chaplet (garland) of grace upon your head and chains and pendants [of gold worn by kings] for your neck. My son, if sinners entice you, do not consent.
>
> —PROVERBS 1:8–10

Then Samson made matters worse. He became angry with his wife, and he left her to return to live with his parents. They should have told him, "Go back to your wife." But they let him live with them for four months. Then he lusted for his wife, so he went back to Timnah with a gift and demanded to sleep with her (Judg. 15:1–2). But her father replied, "I thought you didn't want my daughter, so I gave her away."

This time, Samson caught three hundred foxes, twisted their tails together, and lit them with fire. He sent them into the enemy's ready-to-harvest fields (vv. 4–5). Now Samson was out of control. He had an anointing from God, but there was no correction, nobody to chastise him and channel his anointing.

Samson had been anointed to be a leader, but he lacked the character. He had a bad temper. He wasn't disciplined; he was just strong. And he justified his actions: "And Samson said of them, This time shall I be blameless as regards the Philistines, though I do them evil" (Judg. 15:3). In other words, he was saying, "I'm not to blame for what I'm about to do."

People who are trying to operate this way will always justify their wrongdoings. They'll blame it on "what God has said," they'll justify their own sin by exposing someone else's, or they'll blame what they do on others. But a person with a true anointing doesn't retaliate.

Samson retaliated, and the Philistines sought him out. Then, with the jawbone of an ass, he killed a thousand men (Judg. 15:9–17). Samson was a judge of Israel, a man separated to God from birth. But because he had no one speaking truth into his life, his actions grew progressively more disobedient. Next, he traveled to Gaza and slept with a prostitute there. Nobody told him, "You can't do that—you're a Nazirite!"

Last of all, he got "set up" with Delilah.

Son of Achan

In Joshua 7, read the story of how the Israelites were defeated at Ai and how Joshua traced the cause of the defeat to a man named Achan.

1. What was the primary cause for the humiliating defeat of the Israelites?

☐ Pride

☐ Sin in the camp

☐ Getting out of the will of God

2. To whom did God reveal the problem (vv. 10–12)?

_____

3. Why didn't God tell everybody at the same time—or warn the sinner ahead of time?

_____

_____

4.   The people of Israel were supposed to be unified as they went into battle. To a man, they were supposed to obey the rules about the spoil. What were the rules (v. 11)?

_____

_____

5.   What did Achan do?

_____

_____

6.   How did he cover up his sin?

_____

_____

7.   How is this similar to a story in the New Testament? (See Acts 5:1–10.)

_____

_____

8.   What was the specific punishment in both stories?

_____

_____

9.   Even though such severe consequences may not be visited on people each time they sin, what does God want us to learn from these true stories?

_____

_____

The Father's Anointing Covers Your Vision

Samson was a mighty man, but he didn't have a covering anointing. You remember the story: Delilah begged him to tell her the reason for his strength, and he kept lying to her. Finally, he yielded. She cut his long hair, which broke the last requirement of his Nazirite vow. (See Judges 16:6–20.) And "Samson did not know that the Lord had departed from him" (v. 20).

Samson jumped up just as he always did, thinking, *I've got power*—but he didn't have it anymore. People do the same thing today—they jump up and preach even though they don't have the anointing anymore. People sing all the right notes in praise, but they aren't anointed anymore. What's worse, people say "amen" to preachers based upon their former anointing. They shout and dance from the residue of the anointing. The devil lets you keep "feeling the anointing" so you believe you still have it. But one day, you are going to try to "shake yourself free," and the presence of the Lord will be gone—and you will be blinded to it.

"The Philistines laid hold of Samson, bored out his eyes, and brought him down to Gaza and bound him with [two] bronze fetters" (v. 21). Samson lost his eyesight. He lost his spiritual discernment. He was supposed to be great in the kingdom, yet he ended up being led around by someone who didn't know God or understand his call. When you become unsubmitted and you reject instruction and avoid correction, you lose your vision, and the devil can lead you into a trap.

> I [the Lord] will instruct you and teach you in the way you should go; I will counsel you with My eye upon you.
> —Psalm 32:8

Getting Personal

When I was a little girl, my mother used to call me in from playing outside and make me just sit down. I might ask, "How long do I have to sit?" But how long wasn't the point. It wasn't for discipline; it was for my protection.

I never knew why she was doing it. But on one occasion, about five minutes after I entered the house, somebody outside was hit by a baseball bat. On another occasion, ten minutes after she sat me down, somebody outside was run over by a car.

Now I understand that my mother could pick up in her spirit when a satanic force was about to hinder or try to destroy the call God had placed on my life. So she protected it.

If I had disobeyed my mother or gone and done things without her knowing where I was, it could have cost my life. It shows that there is a price to pay for the absence of authority, regardless of why the authority isn't there.

Eli's Disaster

Another sad example is Eli, the high priest in Israel who knew that his sons were sleeping with women in the temple, yet he did not correct them. (See 1 Samuel 1–3.) Then God sent young Samuel to Eli, choosing Samuel to receive his spiritual inheritance. Samuel was also set apart under a Nazirite's anointing, and even though Eli was not a good leader, Samuel stayed there because that's where he had been placed.

Your job as a son or daughter is to submit. But if your leader doesn't correct you, then the devil can chase you into a realm where you can operate, but your spirit isn't strong enough to handle the battle. You can go to that level, but you can't fight on it. If you don't have spiritual covering, get desperate to find it. Cry out to God in prayer, "God, send me a teacher, an instructor, someone who will channel this anointing on my life." Without a spiritual parent, you will rise to a high level, but you won't make your destiny. You'll reach a mark, but you won't get all the way to the end. The anointing you are carrying is bigger than you are as a person.

Remember Samson. Think about Uzziah. Don't forget Saul. These are only a few examples; there are many more in the Bible. We need correction because a whole nation could fall if just one person doesn't learn how to stay in submission to God. A whole church could suffer if one person hides from correction.

The spiritual inheritance reserved especially for you is awaiting your full obedience. Will you embrace the greatness God has put within you?

The Essentials

To reach the end of our lives without losing God's anointing, we must walk in complete obedience to God and to our spiritual leaders.

Memory Verse

Purposes and plans are established by counsel.

—Proverbs 20:18

To Your Father

Father in heaven: [Write your own prayer, either asking for better spiritual covering or thanking God that you have it already; in either instance, ask Him to protect you from stepping out from under your covering.]

_____

_____

_____

_____

_____

In the name of Jesus, whose blood covers me, amen.

CHAPTER 9

The Spirit of Truth

*E*veryone who goes to church does not belong to the Father. But when the Spirit of Truth shows up, He separates the wheat from the tares. People who don't belong to God cannot digest truth. It's too much for them. They choke on it. But if you belong to God, even though His Word may be cutting you to the core, your spirit will be saying, "Ouch! God, this hurts! Nevertheless, *yes, Lord...I thank You."*

God can give us a portion and bring His work to completion—but if we don't submit our lives to divine instruction, rebuke, and correction, we will end up shipwrecked in our faith.

> But as for you, continue to hold to the things that you have learned and of which you are convinced, knowing from whom you learned [them]....So that the man of God may be complete and proficient, well fitted and thoroughly equipped for every good work.
>
> —2 Timothy 3:14, 17

What Does the Spirit of Truth Do?

Read John 16:13–15; John 18:37–38; and 2 Timothy 3:16–17.

1.   The Bible is a book that contains God's truth. Why can't we

just read it as we would read any book to determine what the truth is?

_____

_____

2.   What is missing when people try to read or study it as they would any other book?

_____

3.   Whose message does the Spirit give us?

_____

4.   Whose message did Jesus give us? (To what did He come to testify? See John 18:37.)

_____

5.   Who will listen to the message (John 18:37)?

_____

6.   How will we be reminded of the truth when we forget it? (See John 14:26.)

_____

7.   Pilate (and countless others) ask, "What is truth?" (John 18:38). How would you answer that question?

_____

_____

_____

Too many people are waiting for God to lay something "heavy" on them. They have their own ideas about what the Father should do, but they are blind to their own shortcomings. If you can't handle the weight of temptation in your own spirit, you'll never be able to handle the weight of the anointing for someone else. Believe me, the anointing is much heavier than anything the devil can put on you!

Don't talk about getting to your next level in God if you're not letting Him clothe you in righteousness. If you have been working through problems in your marriage, are you still coming to church? Do you still praise Him, or do you just sit in the pew with your lips cocked to the side? If you're working through some things in your finances, do you withhold your tithe? If your kids drove you crazy this week, did you let it affect your relationship with God? Are rivers of living water flowing out of your spirit?

I can just hear God saying, "How can I give you anything greater when you can't handle these light afflictions? What are you doing with what you already have?" The Bible says that persecutions will come because of the Word. (See Mark 4:17.) So if you can't handle what you're going through now, don't look for God to give you more of your divine portion. He is not going to give you anything you can't handle.

Stop panicking every time something doesn't go your way. Be a son. Be a daughter. Stay in the presence of your heavenly Father so you can stay submitted and please Him on earth.

No Spiritual Junk Food

We all eat and drink some kind of spiritual food. The question is, what kind is it?

1. **What does your spirit do?**

☐ Nothing; it's just that invisible part of you that exists.

☐ It connects me with God's Spirit and with fellow human beings.

☐ Nobody knows.

2. What kind of "food and drink" does your spirit need? (You can check more than one box. There is no complete set of correct answers.)

☐ Quiet, rest

☐ Reassurance of love

☐ Confidence and safety

☐ Attention

☐ Excitement

☐ Joy

☐ Companionship

☐ Awe

☐ A sense of being "known"

☐ Other

3. Can your spirit get all the nourishment it needs from going to church? Why or why not?

_____

_____

_____

_____

4. What kinds of "empty calories" do you feed your spirit? (Think about the things you may do to give yourself comfort, satisfaction, joy, peace.)

_____

_____

5. How could you change your spiritual diet for the better?

_____

_____

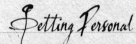

Getting Personal

When I would hear that God can cleanse us and make us pure like Himself, I didn't believe He meant *me!* In fact, I kind of preferred to hear about the people in the Bible who were worse off than I was—they made me feel like I had some company. I figured I would get into heaven, but here on earth I didn't think I'd qualify for much in the way of blessings.

This started to change when I read in John 1 about Nathanael, "an Israelite without guile." It says that Jesus looked into Nathanael's spirit from a distance and saw no falsehood or deceitfulness in him. And Jesus liked that enough to promise some awesome blessings to him, without even being asked.

I thought to myself, *What was Nathanael full of, if he wasn't full of falsehood?* I decided he must have been full of the opposite of falsehood—truth. He must have been just honest. He didn't have to be a PhD or eat locusts to get Jesus' attention. He was just *real.*

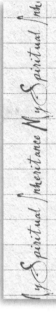

He'd never been introduced to Jesus, so Nathanael asked the obvious question: "How do You know me?" No beating around the bush. He was just plain honest.

Jesus never quite answered his question. But something about the way He related to Nathanael made me want to be "without guile" too, and I realized that the best start would be to tell Him so. When I did, it was as if He walked right up to me and said, "I see you too, and I want you to follow Me now." I actually put my Bible down and stood up.

I'll never stop learning from Him, because I'll never stop following Him. He has changed me. It's like He made "Nathanael" my middle name.

—W. J.

Let your priests be clothed with righteousness (right living and right standing with God); and let Your saints shout for joy!

—Psalm 132:9

Spiritual Racehorses

Racehorses were once wild horses. They are wild horses that have been trained. Wild horses are beautiful, powerful, and have great potential—and they always try to break out, tearing things up in the process.

Their trainers don't start by giving them treats, brushing their coats, and telling them how beautiful they are. They tie a rope around each horse's neck, bring him out of the stall into a fenced area, and start walking. The whole time, the horse is bucking.

Does this sound familiar? Is the Lord leading you, but you are bucking, saying, "Why can't I go out and preach? Why can't I do this or that?" Just keep quiet and keep walking, because you're still wild. God is training you to walk, and you're still galloping, rearing up, and complaining about what you're going through.

The hardest part comes when the trainer clamps a bit in the horse's mouth. The horse literally goes crazy, because he doesn't like anything controlling his mouth. The trainer, on the other hand, understands, "If you let me control your mouth, then when you're running a race, you can be directed around anything that gets in the way. You can get past your struggle, past your opponent, and beyond anything that's trying to hold you captive. I can teach you how to win the prize."

Before putting on a saddle, the next step is to throw blankets on the horse's back. When the trainer throws on the first blanket, the horse bucks, because he doesn't want anything on his back. Like half-broken horses, we may be bucking against instruction, protesting, "Oh, God has a great business for me. He has a great ministry for me." Meantime, you can't tolerate even one blanket on your back.

Being faithful to God is your first blanket. Integrity in your relationships is your second, and so on. Once the blankets are in place, the horse can be saddled. It can never become a winner without submitting to this process, no matter how uncomfortable the process gets.

So don't get upset when God appears to be "breaking" you. If you're going to win the race (receive and activate your spiritual inheritance), you have to be willing to be trained. You're not just a field horse. You're a thoroughbred from a royal family line.

If you want to see heaven opened, if you want your divine portion, you don't need a prophecy from someone. When your life is full of integrity, heaven will open.

The Essentials

Allow God to train you in righteousness so that you can carry the anointing He gives you.

Memory Verse

Jesus stood and said in a loud voice, "If anyone is thirsty, let him come to me and drink. Whoever believes in me, as the Scripture has said, streams of living water will flow from within him." By this he meant the Spirit.

—JOHN 7:37–39, NIV

To Your Father

Father, send Your Spirit to me, and teach me how to drink deeply. I ask You to open the floodgates of heaven and sweep away [list the blockages and impediments that keep you from receiving your full spiritual inheritance].

_____

_____

Teach Me Your ways, and establish me in righteousness. [Continue this prayer from your heart. What truth is touching your heart?]

_____

_____

_____

In Jesus' precious name, amen.

CHAPTER 10

The Making of a Son

*I*n order to receive an inheritance, you have to be born or adopted into a family and then live respectably within that family. Just being a member of a family does not mean you will receive that inheritance. If you rebel, your parents may leave their inheritance to someone more deserving. In the same way, you must embrace the Truth in order to receive your inheritance in the Royal Family into which you've been born again and adopted. There are some requirements for bearing the name of your Father.

Your spiritual leaders need to embrace the same requirements. We've all been adopted by the King, so we need to stay in a good relationship with Him in order to keep our inheritance. But what happens if you have been anointed but your spiritual leader doesn't have an anointing to be a spiritual father to you? How can you remain a true son?

This happened to David. Samuel anointed David as king over Israel. It was an anointing for the future, a promise of a spiritual inheritance to kingship that would be his after King Saul was gone. Then David was placed in a position to serve King Saul, even though King Saul was not walking in his anointing as David's spiritual father.

David served under King Saul, always behaving respect-fully (though at a distance after King Saul turned against him). David had learned how to do this from the one who had anointed him—Samuel, who never broke rank even though he had been raised in the temple under Eli, another unfaithful spiritual father. Submission in a relationship between a spiritual parent and a son or daughter is very powerful, whether or not the parent figure does it right.

Many people are thrown for a loop when their leaders are unfaithful or sinful. They don't recognize that the bonds of spiritual relationship are strengthened by the process of walking through both good—*and bad*—with that person. It's the only way authentic relationships can be proven.

Getting Personal

When I was a young man, I became friends with an older man who was a retired pastor. He saw in me something good that my earthly father had not seen, and he wanted me to grow into my potential. I appreciated his encouragement.

As time went on, this man began to urge me to do things that I felt uncomfortable with. I felt he was thrusting me into situations where I might not only fail, but could even end up doing something illegal. I balked, and he became angry with me. We didn't speak to each other for several years.

Meantime, I continued to mature. I can't say that I respected my former friend, but at least I didn't speak against him to others. (To tell the truth, I think I was ashamed of our disagreement. I didn't want people to know about it.)

Eventually, I felt convicted of my part in our broken relationship. I apologized to my spiritual father, and even though he never apologized to me or seemed to realize that he had provoked the conflict, we resumed our father-son relationship. A little less naïve about his weaknesses and

ambitions for me, I let him pour his wisdom and vision into me.

In actual fact, we became a little like Elijah and Elisha. It was not quite as dramatic as seeing heavenly chariots, but when he died, I could almost feel his mantle around my shoulders.

Sometimes I think about how I almost missed it, but God kept me on track, praise His holy name.

—C.P.

A Man After God's Own Heart

In the life of David, we have an example of a full-process relationship. God called David a man after His own heart. This is because, through every experience, David learned how to examine his own heart and submit himself to God. Whether it was with a lion, bear, Goliath, or King Saul, David exemplified being a son of the kingdom.

Samuel was the "spiritual father" of the nation, so when he anointed David, an anointing from the heavenly Father was poured out upon David's life. (See 1 Samuel 16.) David not only received the anointing to become king, but also he received the supernatural ability to become a true son. But again, the problem remained that Saul didn't know how to be his father. Therefore, David had to walk through some kingdom lessons before he could assume the throne. By the same principle, God gives you a father or mother in the earthly realm (usually your pastor), and you must remain a son or daughter—even if your leader is not walking in the anointing to be your father or mother.

Every leader is going through his or her own process of becoming a son or daughter of God. Saul had disobeyed God, and because of his disobedience, he was suffering a penalty when David came along. He was no longer enjoying the fellowship and power of his anointing from Samuel. Then David entered his camp—David, who was walking in obedience to God and whose life demonstrated the power of his anointing. This distressed Saul, for it was a vivid reminder to him of the anointing he had once had in his life.

David, however, kept in mind his heavenly Father's vision in spite of what he was going through with Saul. Like David, we must begin to see leaders as people who are standing in the stead of God and obtain spiritual direction from the relationship regardless of the circumstances.

> Remind people to be submissive to [their] magistrates and authorities, to be obedient, to be prepared and willing to do any upright and honorable work, to slander or abuse or speak evil of no one, to avoid being contentious, to be forbearing (yielding, gentle, and conciliatory), and to show unqualified courtesy toward everybody.
>
> —Titus 3:1–2

Ripping and Tearing

As we learned in chapter five, Saul lost his anointing through disobedience. To review the story, read 1 Samuel 15:10–11, 23–28.

1. What did Samuel's garment represent?

   ☐ The authority of God

   ☐ Priesthood

   ☐ Eldership

2. What was Saul's anointing supposed to enable him to do?

   _____

   _____

   _____

3.   Was Saul's repentance enough to repair the damage he had done to his anointing (vv. 25–26)? Why or why not?

_____

_____

_____

4.   What were the requirements to retain the anointing?

_____

In which critical requirement did Saul fail (v. 23)?

_____

5.   Did the actual anointing get damaged in this unhappy incident?

_____

6.   What happened to the anointing that had been torn from Saul (1 Sam. 15:28; 16:1)?

_____

_____

7.   Did the anointing get carried more worthily by Saul's successor?

_____

8.   How was the one on whom it was bestowed different from Saul?

_____

9.   Can you think of a personal example of a messed-up anointing?

_____

10. What has happened to the one who messed it up?

_____

_____

_____

11. What has happened to the anointing? Has a spiritual son or daughter inherited it? If so, how is that person different from the one who lost the anointing?

_____

_____

_____

Divine Weapons

Saul became David's enemy. But the Bible says that David behaved himself wisely. (See 1 Samuel 18:27–30.) On two different occasions, Saul threw a spear at David, and David escaped—yet he continued to behave respectfully. Regardless of what Saul did, David never got out of order. He learned how to remain under his anointing—because he understood his purpose.

He also understood that he was called to minister to Saul. Whenever the evil spirit of the Lord would start overtaking Saul, David would start ministering. (See 1 Samuel 16:15–23.) When we start seeing the enemy attack the men and women of God whose leadership we're under, we need to start ministering to them in the Spirit realm. This doesn't necessarily mean we will be able to minister in person; David couldn't do that every time. Even when he did, he played the harp; he didn't prophesy directly in words. Some people are anointed for music; some are anointed for other things such as hospitality. When you see your spiritual leader going through something, get into your anointing to minister to them. Remember the "measure of faith" you have been given. This is part of how God makes you into a son or daughter of the kingdom. Stay in your own lane.

Taking this further, we see that when Saul began to pursue David, David was running for his life, and yet he still wouldn't stoop to say, "Saul is out of his mind. He's raging and chasing me." No, he covered Saul and said, "I'm on a private mission, and nobody knows about it but King Saul and me."

There are many things you'll go through with your leadership that aren't for you to tell to anyone. Many times we miss the mark on this. We go around saying, "Let me tell you what he did..." "Let me tell you how she hurt me." This isn't what a true son would do.

Running from King Saul, David fled to the tabernacle at Nob, where he asked the priest Ahimelech for a weapon to use.

> David said to Ahimelech, Do you have at hand a sword or spear? The king's business required haste, and I brought neither my sword nor my weapons with me. The priest said, The sword of Goliath the Philistine, whom you slew in the Valley of Elah, see, it is here wrapped in a cloth behind the ephod; if you will take that, do so, for there is no other here. And David said, There is none like that; give it to me.
>
> —1 SAMUEL 21:8–9

The only weapon they had in the tabernacle was the sword of the giant that David had killed. And David could *have* Goliath's sword because he had fought and won that battle earlier.

When we submit to proper spiritual alignment, strongholds start coming down. And when another enemy pursues us, we'll be able to take up the weapons we have won by faith. For example, have you fought and won the victory over lying? Now you possess a weapon, and the enemy cannot prevail over you in that area of your life. You can stand against the devil because, like David, you can declare, "Through the strength of the Lord, I killed that giant!"

Honor your father and your mother, as the Lord your God commanded you, that your days may be prolonged and that it may go well with you in the land which the Lord your God gives you.

—DEUTERONOMY 5:16

Honor Your Father and Mother

Even though your earthly father and mother may not become your spiritual parents, the way you have handled your attitude toward them affects your ability to honor subsequent authority figures—and it can affect your ability to receive your full portion from God.

Read Deuteronomy 5:16 and Proverbs 20:20.

1.   Often our parents (earthly or spiritual) have made mistakes. Therefore, *merit* must not be the reason for the command to honor them. What is the fundamental reason for doing it?

_____

_____

2.   How is it possible to honor your earthly or spiritual parents in spite of the areas in which you disagree with them? Must you compromise your integrity? Does it count as honor if you simply refrain from damaging their reputations? Remembering the examples of Samuel and David, write some very specific ways in which you can express honor toward your earthly or spiritual parents:

_____

_____

_____

3. "*...that it may go well with you in the land which the Lord your God gives you*" (Deut. 5:16). What is *your* promised land? Expand on it in terms of your earthly existence, present and future, and your eternal existence. (See also 2 Peter 3:13.)

_____

_____

_____

Interceding for Your Spiritual Leaders

Because Saul continued pursuing him, David found it necessary to keep running. But as he ran, he began to receive prophecies about his situation, words such as, "Today, the Lord has delivered the kingdom into your hands." Some people would advise, "So why not take Saul down?" But that is not God's way. Like David, you may have many opportunities to expose your leader's problems. But if you intercede instead, faithfully praying that he or she will reach the goal, you yourself will be rewarded.

Everybody in the body of Christ can pray, "O God, bless the pastor. Bless his finances; touch his family." But somebody has to be able to say, "Father, You revealed this to me, and I'll take it to my grave. But God, let there be a deliverance." The spiritual inheritance, the word that God has ordained for your leader to impart into your life, cannot be hindered by the flesh as long as you remain in your anointing under the covering of obedience. If you will stay under the covering of obedience, you will be demonstrating to God that you are ready to become a real son or daughter.

Another time, David found Saul sleeping. He took Saul's water pitcher and spear and went a safe distance away. Then he revealed his supernatural love of a son for his father-in-the-making. You can read the story in 1 Samuel 26:12–17. Even though Saul was pursuing David to try to take his life, David was still concerned for Saul's life. He was appalled at the lax security around Saul, and he refrained from taking advantage of it. (This illustration speaks of a real truth that we need to heed. Just because our pastor may have a lot of people hanging around, it does not mean that he or she is spiritually protected. Some people hang around for the status of association. Others stay close to their leaders to get credit for exploits.) So from a safe distance, David shouted, "Why then have you not guarded your lord the king?" (1 Sam. 26:15.)

King Saul felt remorseful for his treatment of David. After this event, he declared that he would no longer chase David or try to harm him (v. 21). He blessed David as a son, and the era was ended. David had passed the test. He was ready to abide in his spiritual inheritance.

God is saying today, "I can trust you with the kingdom if I can trust you with My king." Are you ready to become a trustworthy son or daughter of the kingdom and receive your spiritual inheritance?

The Essentials

You will qualify to inherit your anointed portion if you behave respectfully toward the spiritual father or mother that the Lord has established for you.

Memory Verse

I say to myself, "The LORD is my portion; therefore I will wait for him."

—LAMENTATIONS 3:24, NIV

To Your Father

Father, when David was running from Saul, he prayed, "Have mercy on me, O God, have mercy on me, for in you my soul takes refuge. I will take refuge in the shadow of your wings until the disaster has passed" (Ps. 57:1, NIV). [From Psalm 57 or another psalm, choose words that express your deepest feelings to God:]

_____

_____

_____

_____

_____

In the name of Jesus, who saves me, amen.

CHAPTER 11

The Seduction of Jezebel

*W*hatever God is dealing with you about individually isn't just about you. It's bigger than you are. It's bigger than me. The Father's portion is about generations. It's about relationships. God is about *family.*

Our adversary, the devil, has launched a counterattack—the spirit of Jezebel. His goal is to affect much more than one person. The spirit of Jezebel has been dispatched to frustrate the plans of our heavenly Father, to wreak havoc in the church, and to stop God's purposes.

Why is this important to know? If you don't know where the root of a spirit comes from, you will be frustrated for the rest of your life, fighting only the symptoms. This is what the body of Christ has been guilty of doing as it fights "Ahab and Jezebel," not really getting to the originating root of these evil spirits.

The Lineage of Ahab

We can read about Jezebel in the Book of 1 Kings. Her husband, King Ahab, was the product of an evil lineage that started generations earlier with King Jeroboam, whose reign was a constant power struggle against Rehoboam, Solomon's son. In fear of losing his kingdom, Jeroboam manipulated the people of God under his control. He constructed "high places" and led the entire nation into idolatry. (See 1 Kings 12–14.)

After Jeroboam died, his son Nadab assumed the throne of Israel—walking in his father's ways—until he was killed by one of his subjects, Baasha. Baasha reigned for twenty-four years and destroyed everyone in the house of Jeroboam, but he "walked in the way of Jeroboam and in his sin" (1 Kings 15:34). When Baasha died, his son Elah reigned until he was killed by one of his subjects, Zimri. Zimri held the throne for only seven days, and the people rose up against him and appointed another king—Omri, captain of the army. Upon becoming king, Omri reigned for twelve years, and the Bible says he "did evil in the eyes of the Lord, even worse than all who were before him. He walked in all the ways of Jeroboam" (1 Kings 16:25–26).

Then Omri's son Ahab took the throne, and sin multiplied. He married Jezebel, a king's daughter, and immediately began to serve and worship Baal, the god of her fathers (v. 31). During his twenty-two-year reign, "Ahab did more to provoke the Lord, the God of Israel, to anger than all the kings of Israel before him" (v. 33). The false anointing came into its fullness.

> Notwithstanding I have a few things against thee, because thou sufferest that woman Jezebel, which calleth herself a prophetess, to teach and to seduce my servants to commit fornication, and to eat things sacrificed unto idols. And I gave her space to repent of her fornication; and she repented not. Behold, I will cast her into a bed, and them that commit adultery with her into great tribulation, except they repent of their deeds.
>
> —REVELATION 2:20–22, KJV

The Lineage of Jezebel

Jezebel's father was the high priest of Ashtoreth. His name was Ethbaal, which means "Baal's man." Historically speaking, if a man was a priest in the Old Testament, his children were also raised in the priesthood and were taught the same passion of worship toward the gods that they served. Now we can see why Jezebel was so evil. She was raised in evil; therefore, she had a passion to operate in perversion. The last three letters of her name are not spelled exactly like Baal, but the names *Baal* and *Bel* could be used interchangeably.

This is a clue for us—Jezebel is controlled by a ruling spirit. For years, the church has pointed the finger and declared, "It's the Jezebel spirit." We've lived under the illusion that Jezebel is the controller, when, in fact, Jezebel is the decoy the devil has been using to shift our focus and confuse us.

Motives

Jezebel is given a foothold in the church when people operate out of ungodly motives and thereby disobey the Spirit of the Lord.
Read James 1:13–27.

1. Can we blame the devil for our sinfulness?

_____

Where do our ungodly motives originate (vv. 14–15)?

_____

2. We see here a sort of "genealogy" of sin. What three "generations" do we see here (vv. 14–15)?

_____

_____

_____

3. What has God provided to enable us to be free from sinfulness? (What key word occurs in verses 18, 22, and 23?)

_____

4.   James gives some unambiguous advice about how to resist sinful motives. List several of his specific commands to believers:

_____

_____

_____

_____

5.   The man who merely looks at his reflection in the mirror is guilty of what kind of disobedience?

_____

Is this an *active* (doing something) or a *passive* (doing nothing) sort of disobedience?

_____

What is the cure for this problem?

_____

The Origin of Baal

First Kings 16:33 says, "And Ahab made an Asherah.... Ahab did more to provoke the Lord than all the kings of Israel that were before him."

This verse reveals what really provoked the Lord. It wasn't simply the fact that Ahab had married Jezebel. What provoked the Lord is that he had erected a statue (an idolatrous image) called an *Asherah*. An Asherah was comprised of images of the Ashtoreth goddess, and it was placed in a grove near Baal's altar. Ashtoreth is the female counterpart of Baal. The religion that developed around them was self-centered and perverted; men and women sought lewd pleasures and followed their own wills.

In the present day, the spirit of Ashtoreth is manifested when we are *self-willed*. The corporate (collective) form of Ashtoreth is called Ashtaroth. The spirit of Ashtaroth will transform itself into a common form such as a snake, pig, cow, man, or woman, so the worship becomes snake worship, pig worship, cow worship, and, if it is a human being, it would be called Jezebel. Each of these manifestations masks the real stronghold, which is Ashtaroth. Ashtaroth was the only goddess regarded as being on an equal footing with the male divinities. This means that the spirit can be either male or female, with the ability to switch genders depending on what the job requires.

Whenever anything else is on the throne of our hearts besides God, that thing becomes an object of worship for that individual, church, or region. It becomes the Baal of our life. Anything that God says *no* to, and we say *yes* to, becomes our god. Then we are no different from the people who worshiped Baal. According to 1 Corinthians 6:19, we are temples of the Holy Ghost. Yet when we allow something to become a god in our lives, we have done exactly what they did in the Old Testament. We have now erected an Asherah pole! There is no longer a free flow of God's Spirit in our temples because we are no longer temples of the Holy Spirit.

Trees by Living Water

When God compares the righteous person to a tree planted by living water, He is giving us a vivid and encouraging image. Such trees do not wither or fail to bear fruit in season. How different from the grove in which the Asherah pole is planted!

Read Jeremiah 17:8 and Psalm 1:1–3.

1. What is the source of the righteous man's strength?

_____

2. Jeremiah did not have the benefit of seeing this image at first. Read Jeremiah 12:1–4. Have you ever wondered the same thing?

_____

3. How does Jeremiah 17:8 provide a good response to the complaint in Jeremiah 12:1–4?

_____

_____

4. From Psalm 1:1–3, list several of the actions of the man that show his righteousness:

_____

_____

_____

5. Do you know what it feels like to be "like a tree planted by streams of living water"? If not, what do you think you could do differently to make this your experience?

_____

_____

_____

_____

Elijah

God began His plan for removing the original Jezebel by working through the prophet Elijah. We can learn from his experience.

When it was time for this wicked dynasty to end, King Ahab was the first to die. His death came as the result of his wicked attempt to steal the property—and spiritual inheritance—of Naboth, who owned a vineyard that the king coveted. Jezebel devised a plan for her husband and executed the order to have Naboth killed. When she told Ahab that Naboth was dead, "he arose to go down to the vineyard of Naboth the Jezreelite to take possession of it" (1 Kings 21:16).

> Then the word of the Lord came to Elijah the Tishbite, saying, Arise, go down to meet Ahab king of Israel in Samaria. He is in the vineyard of Naboth, where he has gone to possess it. Say to him, Thus says the Lord: Have you killed and also taken possession? Thus says the Lord: In the place where dogs licked the blood of Naboth shall dogs lick your blood, even yours. And Ahab said to Elijah, Have you found me, O my enemy?
>
> And he answered, I have found you, because you have sold yourself to do evil in the sight of the Lord. See [says the Lord], I will bring evil on you and utterly sweep away and cut off from Ahab every male, bond and free, and will make your household like that of Jeroboam son of Nebat and like the household of Baasha son of Ahijah, for the provocation with which you have provoked Me to anger and made Israel to sin. Also the Lord said of Jezebel: The dogs shall eat Jezebel by the wall of Jezreel. Any belonging to Ahab who dies in the city the dogs shall eat, and any who dies in the field the birds of the air shall eat. For there was no one who sold himself to do evil in the sight of the Lord as Ahab did, incited by his wife Jezebel.
>
> —1 KINGS 21:17–25

Ahab's death sentence was carried out when he was mortally wounded in battle against Syria. The floor of his chariot flowed with his blood. When the battle ended, his men washed the blood out of Ahab's chariot "by the pool of Samaria, where the harlots bathed, and the dogs licked up his blood, as the Lord had predicted" (1 Kings 22:38).

Getting Personal

I have been part of two churches that had trouble with a Jezebel spirit.

The first one was my church when I was growing up. I wasn't old enough to understand what happened there, but my mother told me that it started when certain people in the church began to talk about problems. The leadership, however, didn't want to grapple with the issues they raised. Some of the people who were raising the issues were called "Jezebels," but my mother felt that it was the other way around—that some kind of religious spirit took over some of the leadership, and it showed in the way they handled the dissension. The pastor and his leaders' team were rigid and unloving, and it seemed like nobody could talk to them without getting confused.

My family stayed there for quite a while, but eventually we were so tired of endless conflict that we left and found another church.

In our new church, we had a pastor who was wise and discerning. He said he had learned some things the hard way when, early in his pastorate (when he was "wet behind the ears") some old-timers had tried to change his mind about the direction he was taking the church. They tried to intimidate him and make him worry about whether or not he was doing a good job as a pastor. They were much older than he was, and they really didn't like it when he preached about submission to authority. He was somewhat intimidated, but he stood his ground and handled it like a good strong father would—lots of communication, lots of prayer, and some discipline. Finally, some of the old-timers got so fed up that they left. It seemed like a shame at first, but everything calmed down and began to move forward.

We came along about ten years after the dust had settled, and we watched this pastor, who by now was a seasoned man of God, nip other potential situations in the beginning stages. It seems like anyplace where the Spirit of God is doing a good work, the devil is prowling around trying to bring it down. I know that my part is to stay close to God and to keep my relationships strong—and I pray for my pastor to continue to be a wise leader.

—P. F.

Jezebel Enters Through Relinquished Authority

Jezebel cannot rule where she hasn't been given authority. But she will assume authority through anyone—male or female, Jew or Gentile, minister or lay person—who gives her that authority. In this way her actions are legal, and she knows that she cannot be denounced, dethroned, or rebuked because she did not take over—she was *given* the power.

How does a believer give her that authority? By being passive in the things of God—disobedient to your assignment and calling. For example, let's say that God told you to sing, and you said, "I don't feel like singing." At that moment, Jezebel would say to Ashtaroth, "I'll sing," and joins the choir. Jezebel enters in wherever a person in the church is walking in disobedience. In all of this, it *looks* like God is still getting the glory. It is a "form" of godliness that denies God's power.

People who are influenced by Ashtaroth can be very dishonest and manipulative. This chief spirit is a liar, just like her father, Satan. Therefore, the spirit will lie, cheat, steal, and manipulate—but the minute you identify and confront it, this spirit starts to act spiritual, prophesying and speaking in tongues. This deceptive spirit copies the anointing and tries to hide as it continues to pervert what the Word of the Lord has established.

Ashtaroth rarely adopts the same appearance twice, so our obedience must be absolute. We cannot give place to the devil (Eph. 4:27). If we know the Word of God and fail to do what we know, we can become prey to this spirit. If we forget our God-given authority in Christ, Jezebel can take over. She will assume a place of authority and begin giving birth to her wicked fruits in our lives.

We have been foolish enough to diminish Jezebel in our thinking to being one sister in the church, daubed in makeup, who is after the pastor. We think she is just one person who is sowing disunity. Jezebel is a lot bigger than that. She is not after the local church as much as she is after the corporate anointing and the End-Time plan of God.

This is real. We must not be ignorant or passive about this deceptive spirit. We must walk boldly into our spiritual inheritance!

Taking Out the Plank

> Why do you look at the speck of sawdust in your brother's eye and pay no attention to the plank in your own eye? How can you say to your brother, "Let me take the speck out of your eye," when all the time there is a plank in your own eye? You hypocrite, first take the plank out of your own eye, and then you will see clearly to remove the speck from your brother's eye.
>
> —MATTHEW 7:3–5, NIV

It's too easy to point the finger everywhere but at yourself, when that's the place we need to check first when we're looking for the evil one. Read the following list of Jezebel's characteristics, and note where you have seen such behavior in yourself. If it is current behavior, stop now and ask the Lord if you need to deal with disobedience in your life. This is serious business.

JEZEBEL	I SEE THIS IN MYSELF...
1. Is a seducing spirit	
2. Makes excuses for her behavior	
3. Hates civility	
4. Hates repentance and holiness	
5. Gives false prophetic words, dreams, and visions	
6. Is a tyrant	
7. Changes the rules; feels above the law	
8. Pretends to love; uses people's weakness against them	
9. Creates division and conflict	
10. Discredits others' integrity	
11. Is proud	
12. Calls herself a prophet or prophetess	
13. Accuses true prophets falsely	
14. Lacks humility; brags about her giftedness	
15. Has personal problems, but hides them	
16. Seems genuine, but is spiritually "off"	
17. Likes to control money	
18. Is sarcastic and derogatory	
19. Is anxious; has no peace or joy	
20. Is full of plans that go nowhere	
21. Pretends to be a worshiper or intercessor	
22. Aligns herself with true prophets for credibility	
23. Brings confusion wherever she goes	
24. Brings a slumbering spirit wherever she goes	
25. Brings complacency and apathy upon the body	

> Jehu lifted up his face to the window and said, Who is on
> my side? Who? And two or three eunuchs looked out at him.
> And he said, Throw her down! So they threw her down, and
> some of her blood splattered on the wall and on the horses,
> and he drove over her.
>
> —2 Kings 9:32–33

We Must Become a Company Coming

How is the church going to destroy Jezebel? How are we going to
dismantle that spirit? We have to become "a company coming."

> So Jehu son of Jehoshaphat, the son of Nimshi, conspired
> against Joram [to dethrone and slay him]....So Jehu rode
> in a chariot and went to Jezreel....A watchman on the
> tower in Jezreel spied the company of Jehu as he came, and
> said, I see a company.
>
> 2 Kings 9:14, 16–17

In other words, when we're in church, one person can't be saying, "God wants us to go on a twenty-one-day fast," while another
is saying, "We need to pray more about it," and yet another person
says, "Why does it have to be twenty-one days? Why can't it be five
days?" There's no order in that. Divine order must flow through
strong leadership.

When it is time for us to become "a company coming," we
must respond like warhorses—charging toward the enemy as one.
That's how the church leaders in the Book of Acts ministered unto
the Lord in order to receive His direction. They stopped talking,
started seeking, and kept obeying. And they did it in unity. That
gave no place to the devil.

As the people of God, we have to come against Jezebel as a
united company of believers so she cannot find a corner to whisper

in. When she looks to the left or to the right, we'll be saying, "Holy." When she looks at the praise team, she'll hear, "Holy." The spirit of Jezebel will not be able to find a place of activation.

Jezebel knows the mighty warriors in the Spirit. She knows the choir that's going to sing until demons run out of the church. She knows the intercessors who are going to drive the enemy out. And she knows the man of God who is going to take the people to another level in God—stirring them to rise up like mighty giants in the Spirit.

"Now when Jehu came to Jezreel, Jezebel heard of it, and she painted her eyes and beautified her head and looked out of [an upper] window" (v. 30). When it's time for Jezebel to die, she'll try to change her appearance, like a chameleon, to look more beautiful. She suddenly starts acting sweet and kind: "Oh, I love you." "God bless you." But God will say, "I still see you, Jezebel. You're the same demon, even though you painted your eyes and beautified yourself." If we have spiritual vision, we can see past the surface and expose the enemy.

> Will evildoers never learn—
> > those who devour my people as men eat bread
> > and who do not call on the Lord?
> There they are, overwhelmed with dread,
> > for God is present in the company of the righteous.
> > > —PSALM 14:4–5, NIV

Armed and Dangerous

The church must be united and ready for the inevitable encounter with evil, and each believer needs to be prepared for the fight. As in any armed conflict, each soldier needs to be ready, but the battle cannot be won unless the company of soldiers works together.
Read Ephesians 6:10–18.

1.   Who forged this armor?

_____

Who straps it on?

_____

2.   What will happen to pacifist or fearful soldiers who refuse to don their armor?

_____

3.   List the six components of the armor of God:

_____

_____

_____

_____

_____

_____

4.   Choose one piece of the armor, and write about how it is more effective against an invading army if other armed soldiers are standing firm side by side:

_____

_____

5.   How do we know what to do in the battle? How do we keep in touch with the Commander (v. 18)?

_____

_____

Jezebel Must Fall

The Holy Spirit is calling the church to grow up. We must come to maturity so that we can be part of a mighty company that carries out the vision God has given to our spiritual parents.

In order to reach spiritual maturity, we must cry out to God and say, "God, my heart isn't right before You. Help me get to the place in You where I'm walking, talking, and living right." Take inventory of your motives. It must be the Lord who is leading you to step into destiny. Your personal vision must support the vision of the man or woman God is using to build His church. Our purpose—no matter what kind of portion He has given us—is to build His kingdom. The church isn't about *you*; it's not about *me*; it's much bigger than any one of us.

Activate your measure of faith in the Lord, so He can help you to finish your course. God is getting His house in order. Your portion is being united with others to fulfill His purpose.

The Essentials	Your spiritual inheritance is part of a corporate anointing. Therefore, you must learn how to resist the spirit of Jezebel.

Memory Verse	Submit yourselves, then, to God. Resist the devil, and he will flee from you. —James 4:7, niv

To Your Father

My Father in heaven, I want to be numbered as part of the company of the faithful. I want to be walking, talking, and living right. I want to have true spiritual vision. I don't want to lag behind You either, passive and unaware of the dangers. I want to resist the temptation to run ahead of You, Lord, which would allow Jezebel to have entrance into my church.

Here is what I am learning about my motives and about how I can fit into Your plan for Your church:

_____

_____

_____

_____

Take care of me, Lord, in the midst of the perils that surround me. I trust in You. Amen.

CHAPTER 12

Babylon's Fall

*J*ezebel may be wreaking havoc in the kingdom, but a day of reckoning is coming. Jezebel (Ashtaroth) has a thirst for power. This ancient enemy will continue to try to recapture and abuse the most sacred things in the church.

But if we, God's people, will walk in our true inheritance, Jezebel cannot usurp our God-given authority. Jesus has freed us from the curse of this deceptive spirit. As we walk in covenant authority by submitting to the order of the Lord, He will restore the kingdom through us.

Remember, Astharoth was birthed out of Babylon. Again, this parallels the entrance of Ashtaroth into the kingdom of Israel when Ahab married Jezebel and submitted to the gods of her fathers (1 Kings 16:30–33).

But in the end, Babylon is going to fall—God Himself will judge her.

> And he shouted with a mighty voice, She is fallen! Mighty Babylon is fallen! She has become a resort and dwelling place for demons, a dungeon haunted by every loathsome spirit, an abode for every filthy and detestable bird.
>
> —REVELATION 18:2

When Babylon goes down, every demon spirit will live there. Here we are, chasing demon spirits and binding "symptoms," but our real enemy is Babylon, their demonic stronghold. Each demon has a specific manifestation (lust, pride, and so on), but from these verses in Revelation we learn that Ashtaroth (symbolized by her birthplace, Babylon) is at the core of each manifestation. This passage tells us that in the end all demons are going back "home" to her. Babylon is their dwelling place.

Most Sacred Things

Read Leviticus 23:37–38; 1 Corinthians 3:17; and Colossians 2:16–17.

1. In the Old Testament, what made something "sacred"?

_____

_____

2. In the New Testament, what makes something "sacred"?

_____

_____

3. What is the danger of valuing sacred objects and rituals?

_____

_____

4. Name several underlying qualities of sacredness.

_____

_____

_____

5. In your experience, how does Satan try to usurp or counterfeit these particular qualities?

_____

_____

False Bride

Babylon is a false bride with a false inheritance.

Jesus has a true bride through whom He moves in the earth. The devil tries to copy this, flaunting his false bride with her stolen inheritance.

But our God is mighty. Babylon's evil ministry is going to come back on her. When Jezebel died, dogs ate her flesh. By the time Jehu sent men to get her body, all that remained were her skull, palms, and feet (2 Kings 9:34–35). Even this confirmed her counterfeit anointing. It's the copy of Moses' anointing of Aaron as high priest; after pouring oil over Aaron's head, Moses slaughtered a bull and two rams. He placed the blood of the second ram on Aaron's right ear, right thumb, and right big toe, then on the head, hand, and foot of his sons (Lev. 8:12, 23–24).

On every level, this spirit is a copycat. But in the end, just like the beast on which she rides, Babylon will be consumed with fire.

> But as for me, my feet had almost slipped;
>> I had nearly lost my foothold.
> For I envied the arrogant
>> when I saw the prosperity of the wicked.
>> —Psalm 73:2–3, NIV

False Prosperity

1. Babylon wars against the church by parading the things she loves. Give some examples of the types of things that Babylon loves:

_____

_____

_____

2. Have you seen some of the "parade" going by? Give an example of what you have seen:

_____

_____

_____

3. What makes prosperity evil?

_____

_____

4. Is all prosperity evil?

_____

5. How can you be sure that your own desire for prosperity is in line with God's kingdom?

_____

_____

True Bride

After Babylon falls, the saints will rise in splendor and majesty! Their true inheritance is righteousness, our Father's character. It is "dazzling and white." Babylon will never have any part of it.

> Then from the throng there came a voice, saying, Praise our God, all you servants of His, you who reverence Him, both small and great! After that I heard what sounded like the shout of a vast throng, like the boom of many pounding waves, and like the roar of terrific and mighty peals of thunder, exclaiming, Hallelujah (praise the Lord)! For now the Lord our God the Omnipotent (the All-Ruler) reigns! Let us rejoice and shout for joy [exulting and triumphant]! Let us celebrate and ascribe to Him glory and honor, for the marriage of the Lamb [at last] has come, and His bride has prepared herself. She has been permitted to dress in fine (radiant) linen, dazzling and white—for the fine linen is (signifies, represents) the righteousness (the upright, just, and godly living, deeds, and conduct, and right standing with God) of the saints (God's holy people).
>
> —REVELATION 19:5–8

Bridal Garments

Babylon was like a false bride with an insatiable desire for costly goods, power, and influence. Her counterpart today can be seen in the religious spirits who want to control the church. But the false bride cannot touch the true inheritance of the people of God.

Read Revelation 19:7–8.

1.   What does the fine linen stand for?

2.   What did the bride do before the wedding?

_____

3.   Applying this to your own life, what do you think this means?

_____

_____

4.   How does the linen garment relate to our true inheritance as
sons and daughters of God?

_____

_____

～～～～～～～～～～～～～～～～～～～～～～

Even now, it is time to rise up and take what rightfully belongs
to us! We must keep moving forward, clothed with the Lord Jesus
Christ; no weapon formed against us shall prosper.

For the Lord God is a Sun and Shield; the Lord bestows
[present] grace and favor and [future] glory (honor, splendor, and heavenly bliss)! No good thing will He withhold
from those who walk uprightly. O Lord of hosts, blessed
(happy, fortunate, to be envied) is the man who trusts in
You [leaning and believing in You, committing all and
confidently looking to You, and that without fear or mis-
giving]! Lord, You have [at last] been favorable and have
dealt graciously with Your land [of Canaan]; You have
brought back [from Babylon] the captives of Jacob. You
have forgiven and taken away the iniquity of Your people,
You have covered all their sin.

—PSALM 84:11–85:2

The Essentials

Regardless of how impressive Babylon appears to be, she will fall, taking all that she represents with her.

Memory Verse

For the Lord God is a sun and shield;
  the Lord bestows favor and honor;
no good thing does he withhold
  from those whose walk is blameless.
—Psalm 84:11, NIV

To Your Father

Father God, I bow before You in holy awe. I bring You everything I have, all my possessions, all my virtues, and all my sins. [Name a few specific ones.]

_____

_____

_____

I do not want to participate in anything evil, even when it masquerades as goodness. Please show me the difference, and help me to repent quickly when I make mistakes. I pray in the name of Jesus, amen.

CHAPTER 13

The Real Authority

We will have real authority in Jesus Christ as we live in obedience to the Holy Spirit. As we learn from the example of Jesus when He walked on earth, yielding is the only way to obtain and maintain our dominion over the enemy. Yielding keeps us in a posture of true sonship in Christ, where we have our expected inheritance.

If you have opened the door through disobedience and let Jezebel in, rebuking the devil isn't going to change a thing. But when you yield your life to God, He'll throw the authority of Jezebel down. It is a *life* that throws her down—not *talk*.

When you're obedient to the Lord, you don't have to worry about rebuking the devil. And you don't have to fight with Jezebel. James 4:7 says, "So be subject to God. Resist the devil [stand firm against him], and he will flee from you."

Submit and resist. When you yield to the Lord, the authority of God will cast Satan out.

Through Jesus

Read Hebrews 12:2 and Philippians 3:14.

1. Where do these scriptures encourage us to fix our attention?

Why should we do this?

_____

2. **What is another name for our eternal inheritance?**

_____

3. **Who gives us faith?**

_____

4. **Is faith given to us in a mature form? How do you know? What is happening to our faith as we live our lives?**

_____

_____

_____

God Maintains His Power

God foreknew that the powers of darkness would fight to keep His eternal plan from coming to pass. But since He's the real authority, no power in heaven, on earth, or under the earth can resist Him. From the beginning of mankind, God has been saying, "You must follow Me. You must follow My ways. You must do things My way." There is no other way to reach destiny.

To receive our full inheritance as sons and daughters of the kingdom, we have to come through Jesus Christ—the real authority—the prime example of sonship. Before He created time, God knew that He would look down upon creation and be grieved at the state of man, so He made provision to do something about it.

Our heavenly Father foresaw mankind's need for a redeemer, and His Son Jesus said, "Father, here I am…send Me." He willingly gave up the glory of heaven to come and give us an eternal inheritance. Because Jesus was uncompromisingly righteous, you can live in right standing with God. *That's real authority!*

> Who hath believed our report? and to whom is the arm of the LORD revealed?...Surely he hath borne our griefs, and carried our sorrows: yet we did esteem him stricken, smitten of God, and afflicted. But he was wounded for our transgressions, he was bruised for our iniquities: the chastisement of our peace was upon him; and with his stripes we are healed. All we like sheep have gone astray; we have turned every one to his own way; and the LORD hath laid on him the iniquity of us all....Yet it pleased the LORD to bruise him; he hath put him to grief: when thou shalt make his soul an offering for sin, he shall see his seed, he shall prolong his days, and the pleasure of the LORD shall prosper in his hand. He shall see of the travail of his soul, and shall be satisfied: by his knowledge shall my righteous servant justify many; for he shall bear their iniquities.
>
> —ISAIAH 53:1, 4–6, 10–11, KJV

Through Samaria

Jesus went through Samaria to reverse the curse of Ahab and Jezebel. Samaria was the place from which they had once ruled over Israel. (See 1 Kings 16:29.) We remember the story of Jesus meeting the Samaritan woman at the well:

> It was necessary for Him to go through Samaria. And in doing so, He arrived at a Samaritan town called Sychar...and Jacob's well was there. So Jesus, tired as He was from His journey, sat down [to rest] by the well....Presently, when a woman of Samaria came along to draw water, Jesus said to her, Give Me a drink—for His disciples had gone off into the town to buy food—The Samaritan woman said to

Him, How is it that You, being a Jew, ask me, a Samaritan [and a] woman, for a drink?—For the Jews have nothing to do with the Samaritans—Jesus answered her, If you had only known and had recognized God's gift and Who this is that is saying to you, Give Me a drink, you would have asked Him [instead] and He would have given you living water.

She said to Him, Sir, You have nothing to draw with [no drawing bucket] and the well is deep; how then can you provide living water?... Jesus answered her, All who drink of this water will be thirsty again. But whoever takes a drink of the water that I will give him shall never, no never, be thirsty any more.... Go, call your husband and come back here.

The woman answered, I have no husband. Jesus said to her, You have spoken truly in saying, I have no husband. For you have had five husbands, and the man you are now living with is not your husband.

John 4:4–11, 13–14, 16–18

"It was necessary for Him to go through Samaria"—not for geographical reasons, because Jews usually avoided going through Samaria to travel between Judea and Galilee. It was necessary for Jesus to go through Samaria because He needed to fulfill His Father's will.

This Samaritan woman was with her sixth man. Evil Ahab had become king of Israel in Samaria after six previous kings. In other words, Ahab was the seventh king over the divided kingdom of Israel. In a similar way, Jesus was the Seventh Man to this woman. He canceled the wicked lineage and perfected God's preordained plan. Jesus dealt with the spirit of Jezebel—through a single woman who dared to be obedient.

Walk in My Ways

Thus says the Lord of hosts: If you will walk in My ways and keep My charge, then also you shall rule My house and have charge of My courts, and I will give you access [to My presence] and places to walk among these who stand here....For behold, I will bring forth My servant the Branch....Behold (look at, keep in sight, watch) the Man [the Messiah] whose name is the Branch, for He shall grow up in His place and He shall build the [true] temple of the Lord.

—ZECHARIAH 3:7–8; 6:12

1. Who is the Branch?

_____

2. What is the significance of the title "Branch"? (You will have to be a detective. Read Jeremiah 33:15; Ezekiel 17:22–24; Isaiah 9:7.)

_____

_____

3. What did Jesus say about *you* being a branch? (Copy John 15:5, and then write your thoughts.)

_____

_____

_____

_____

Getting Personal

I've been getting back to basics. After a long time of involvement with spiritual warfare, binding and loosing, breaking curses, fasting and praying, I realized that I had started to become almost like my own savior. I was intense. I was anxious. I was taking too much responsibility for remembering all the strategies of the kingdom. I was forgetting that Jesus had done it all already and that all I had to do was obey Him!

I don't mean to say that all of those measures are worthless. But they are worthless if they're detached from an obedient response to the Spirit of the Son of God. The Bible says that the Holy Spirit will remind us of all truth. I'm glad He reminded me of that one.

–Y. M.

Jesus, Our Ultimate Example

Jesus, our ultimate example of sonship, went through a process. He started out with the Father in heavenly places and was sent out from the Father to earth. (He was sent; He didn't just go.) Jesus was sent out from heaven to fulfill the vision and will of the Father. His "food" was to do the will of His Father (John 4:34). The rest of the process was completed as He agonized in the Garden of Gethsemane and was marched from judgment hall to judgment hall before He was crucified.

During the early parts of His ministry, Jesus walked in the glorified state of being recognized as the Son of God because of the miracles He performed. In the end, He was recognized as the Son of God who, no matter how much He was brutalized, would never deny His Father in heaven. When Jesus completed the divine process as the Son of God, He said, "All authority (all power of rule) in heaven and on earth has been given to Me" (Matt. 28:18). And it truly was.

Everybody today wants to stand in the pulpit and preach, lay hands on the sick, cast out devils, and get the accolades of the public. But when it's time for sonship to be proven, will you deny Christ? Will you throw in the towel? When everything you know is being tested and tried, and you feel like your whole world is falling apart, will you still stand and say, "Nevertheless, I will do my Father's will. Not my will, Lord, but Thy will be done"?

If God is for you (and He is), who can be against you? If God is for you, can you embrace submission and obedience? Can you trust God to order your steps and give you counsel through a spiritual father on earth? Can you trust Him in everything, even though you can't see what may happen tomorrow?

I said earlier that a spiritual father sees who you are to become. When a leader recognizes the calling of God on someone's life, there's something about that person's presence that satisfies the leader's spiritual intuition. And he knows this son or daughter will go through a process in the physical realm. There will always be a process.

Sometimes when I meet people, I'll see a glory cloud resting on them. This not only reveals a higher anointing upon them to do mighty works, but it means that the same anointing will preserve them through the process. God has already foreseen the battles. Many of them will have to face the spirit of death and be confronted by demonic forces from the pit of hell. So the anointing must be as great to sustain them in trials as it will be for them to perform the acts of God.

To repeat: we must become yielded vessels unto God because the authority of God through the anointing defeats the enemy. So when battles come, we can stand in faith knowing that what Jesus did at Calvary will carry us into our destiny.

The Essentials	Jesus is our perfect example of obedient sonship, over whom Satan cannot prevail. Through Him, we obtain our inheritance.

Memory Verse	"My food," said Jesus, "is to do the will of him who sent me and to finish his work."

—JOHN 4:34, NIV

To Your Father

Father God, I come to Jacob's well to meet Your Son. What can I do in obedience to Your will and His? [Pause and listen to the Holy Spirit as He speaks to your heart. Write down what He tells you do.]

_____

_____

_____

_____

You are my Father, and Your Son, Jesus, is my elder Brother. I want to be an obedient son/daughter. Through Him I pray, amen.

CHAPTER 14

Our True Inheritance

o become sons or daughters of the kingdom, we must embrace our Father's character and do what pleases Him. Remember the prodigal son (Luke 15:11–32). He thought the physical part of his earthly inheritance was all his father had to offer. But after leaving his father's house and losing everything, he discovered that physical rewards soon perish.

Like the prodigal son, many of us have left our father's house and stopped using our "measure of faith" to support his vision and build the kingdom. Then we wonder why trouble comes and everything starts falling apart.

Jesus said, "You are the salt of the earth, but if salt has lost its taste (its strength, its quality), how can its saltiness be restored? It is not good for anything any longer but to be thrown out and trodden underfoot by men" (Matt. 5:13). Salt not only enhances the natural flavor of food, but it's also a preservative. In other words, whatever we apply salt to doesn't decay or rot. Our kingdom lineage, which incorporates the inheritance of a "good name" and good character, protects us from the enemy.

> Be strong, alert, and courageous, all you people of the land,
> says the Lord, and work! For I am with you, says the Lord
> of hosts. According to the promise that I covenanted with
> you when you came out of Egypt, so My Spirit stands and

abides in the midst of you; fear not. For thus says the Lord of hosts: Yet once more, in a little while, I will shake and make tremble the [starry] heavens, the earth, the sea, and the dry land; and I will shake all nations and the desire and the precious things of all nations shall come in, and I will fill this house with splendor, says the Lord of hosts, The silver is Mine and the gold is Mine, says the Lord of hosts. The latter glory of this house [with its successor, to which Jesus came] shall be greater than the former, says the Lord of hosts; and in this place will I give peace and prosperity, says the Lord of hosts.

—HAGGAI 2:4–9

Riches

Read Ephesians 1:13–19.

1. How do we know that our inheritance is guaranteed (vv. 13–14)?

_____

2. What two pieces of evidence did Paul cite to show that the Ephesians had accepted their salvation fully (v. 15)?

_____

3. Did this prove that they had "arrived" as perfect Christians? How do you know?

_____

_____

4. What was Paul's persistent prayer for them (vv. 17–19)? Put your answer into a prayer form: "Dear Father: In these people I

see great faith in You and love for each other. I ask that You would give every one of them…

_____

_____

_____

_____

5. According to this scripture, what are at least four of the components of the riches of our inheritance in Christ Jesus?

_____

_____

_____

_____

Getting Personal

I have not found my spiritual father or mother yet, and it's not for a lack of interest or effort. One thing that has held me strongly is Psalm 68:5, which states that God is "a father of the fatherless." He is my ultimate Father, and He can be trusted to take care of me, cover me, and guide me.

On the strength of that conviction, I am making every effort to cooperate with the Holy Spirit as He speaks to me through the Bible, sermons (oftentimes on the radio and TV), and what I read in books and Christian magazines.

I realize that if Samuel could turn out to be such a faithful man of God even though he was raised by Eli, who was undoubtedly not a good father-figure for him (we know that he wasn't a good father to his natural sons, and he made a lot of bad decisions), I have some opportunity to turn out to be a faithful son as well.

Unless the Lord takes me home tomorrow, there's still time to come more completely into alignment with the will of God. He knows that's where my heart is.

—S. V.

Seven Character Traits of God

If being the true salt of the earth entails embracing our Father's character, we need to know what His character consists of. Proper spiritual alignment is critical so He can impart the flow of His anointing to us and restore us.

Seven is the perfect number of God, and we can identify at least seven character traits of our Father.

> For behold, I will bring forth My servant the Branch. For behold, upon the stone which I have set before Joshua, upon that one stone are seven eyes or facets [the all-embracing providence of God and the sevenfold radiations of the Spirit of God].
>
> —Zechariah 3:8–9

The stone represents Jesus, the head of the church:

> Therefore thus says the Lord God, Behold, I am laying in Zion for a foundation a Stone, a tested Stone, a precious Cornerstone of sure foundation; he who believes (trusts in, relies on, and adheres to that Stone) will not be ashamed or give way or hasten away [in sudden panic].
>
> —Isaiah 28:16

The stone which the builders rejected has become the chief cornerstone. This is from the Lord and is His doing; it is marvelous in our eyes.

—PSALM 118:22–23

The Father's character has been "carved" into Jesus, our Rock. As fellow heirs, we can inherit a portion of that character, which is much more important than any temporal inheritance. Only with the traits of character that are birthed by the Holy Spirit (the "sevenfold radiations of God") will we be able to help fulfill the plan of the Lord in this final hour.

The seven eyes (facets) or radiations are described in Isaiah 11:1–3 as seven attributes of our Father. They are:

1. The Spirit of the Lord: "The Spirit of the Lord is upon Me…" (Luke 4:18, KJV).
2. The Spirit of wisdom: "[May] the Father of glory…give unto you the spirit of wisdom…" (Eph. 1:17, KJV).
3. The Spirit of understanding: "A man of understanding is of an excellent spirit" (Prov. 17:27, KJV).
4. The Spirit of counsel: "For I have not shunned to declare unto you all the counsel of God" (Acts 20:27, KJV).
5. The Spirit of might: "But truly I am full of power by the spirit of the LORD, and of judgment, and of might…" (Mic. 3:8, KJV).
6. The Spirit of knowledge: "And he hath filled him with the spirit of God, in wisdom, in understanding, and in knowledge…" (Exod. 35:31, KJV).
7. The Spirit of the reverential and obedient fear of the Lord: "The LORD taketh pleasure in them that fear him" (Ps. 147:11, KJV).

> And there shall come forth a Shoot out of the stock of Jesse [David's father], and a Branch out of his roots shall grow and bear fruit. And the Spirit of the Lord shall rest upon Him—the Spirit of wisdom and understanding, the Spirit of counsel and might, the Spirit of knowledge and of the reverential and obedient fear of the Lord—and shall make Him of quick understanding, and His delight shall be in the reverential and obedient fear of the Lord.
>
> —ISAIAH 11:1–3

Too many people have been trying to operate in the things of the Spirit without the authority, wisdom, understanding, counsel, might, knowledge, and fear of the Lord. It will no longer suffice to rely on our human character. The perfect government of the Lord Jesus Christ is coming to rule in the earth. God is getting His house in order. Powers are being shaken. The enemy's attack has stepped up. The perfecting work of God in His saints has intensified in this spiritual season. We must come into proper spiritual alignment according to the biblical pattern.

> See, the Lion of the tribe of Judah, the Root (Source) of David, has won (has overcome and conquered)! He can open the scroll and break its seven seals! And there between the throne and the four living creatures (ones, beings) and among the elders [of the heavenly Sanhedrin] I saw a Lamb standing, as though it had been slain, with seven horns and with seven eyes, which are the seven Spirits of God [the sevenfold Holy Spirit] Who have been sent [on duty far and wide] into all the earth.
>
> —REVELATION 5:5–6

Strongholds

Joshua led the people of Israel into the Promised Land, winning battle after battle against the strong kings who held the territory. In the same way, Jesus leads the way for us to conquer the strongholds of the enemy in our own lives, making it possible for us to take possession of what is ours by divine right. Like the land of Canaan, we belong to the Lord completely from the moment we are saved, but much of our "territory" is occupied by resistant concepts, habits, thought patterns, expectations, and desires.

Look at the following list of potential strongholds, and note any personal applications that may apply to your life. (This list is far from exhaustive.)

- Unforgiveness

_____

- Bitterness

_____

- Distrust, suspicion

_____

- Doubt

_____

- Control, manipulation

_____

- Vengefulness

_____

- Confusion

_____

- Lust

- Fear

- Anger, being critical

- Addictions, obsessions, fixations

- Dishonesty, denial

- Irresponsibility

- Negativism

- Self-defense

- Pride, self-sufficiency, ambition

- False security

- False beliefs ("I am sickly...unstable...a failure...")

- Prejudice

- Jealousy

- **Other**

_____

_____

At the end of this chapter, you will find a prayer that you can pray to renew your commitment to embrace the freedom that is yours as a child of the King.

By My Spirit

God told Zerubbabel, "Not by might, nor by power, but by My Spirit" (Zech. 4:6). The work of the Lord will prevail in this season—not the wisdom or works of man. The oil of the anointing is flowing directly from the Father through Jesus Christ by the power of the Holy Spirit to strengthen His church.

Your power or ability as a son or daughter to submit to your spiritual parents is going to be possible only through the Holy Spirit. And if you are a spiritual parent, you will only be able to lead by the power of the Holy Ghost. The flesh will profit nothing. Your total ability to either follow or lead will be the result of spiritual union with our Father in heaven.

To continually tap into this supernatural flow, our lives will have to remain pure before the Lord. We have to be led by the Spirit. We must submit to Jesus Christ through the ministry of the Holy Spirit, or life will not flow through us to others.

The oil of the anointing is breaking every yoke of bondage, but the Spirit of the Lord will only break yokes for those who have submitted themselves according to His pattern. You must be a true son or daughter of the kingdom, not a spiritual "lone ranger" with a personal agenda. If you have removed yourself from God's covering through a divinely appointed spiritual father or mother, you have exposed yourself to the enemy.

It's *by the Spirit,* not by human knowledge, wisdom, gifts, or talents. This means the days of spiritual showboating, politicking, name-dropping, and the like are screeching to a halt. Now more than ever, we should be rejoicing in the fact that we're sons and daughters of the gospel. Remember what Jesus said to His disciples:

> Behold! I have given you authority and power to trample upon serpents and scorpions, and [physical and mental strength and ability] over all the power that the enemy [possesses]; and nothing shall in any way harm you. Nevertheless, do not rejoice at this, that the spirits are subject to you, but rejoice that your names are enrolled in heaven.
>
> —Luke 10:19–20

Today's church is so much like the prodigal son. We've taken the physical portion of our inheritance and left our father's house to waste it on our own desires. Our *true inheritance*—the supernatural character of our Father through Jesus Christ and the ministry of the Holy Spirit—is waiting to be restored to us *in the house of our spiritual father.*

God is calling every member of the body of Christ to sonship through the same royal line. By the power of the Holy Spirit, He has made true sons and daughters who can reflect their heavenly Father's image and likeness to the world. When people see God's people, they should see God's character.

The spirit of "fathers" is returning to the earth as leaders are turning to our heavenly Father. As this happens, the orderly flow of the anointing is rising up and breaking every yoke of bondage.

The Essentials

> We must embrace our true inheritance, which is our Father's holiness. Everything else flows from that.

Memory Verse

> And we, who with unveiled faces all reflect the Lord's glory, are being transformed into his likeness with ever-increasing glory, which comes from the Lord, who is the Spirit.
> —2 CORINTHIANS 3:18, NIV

To Your Father

My Father, I want to be more like You. I want to please You by accepting Your help to grow in reflecting Your character. When I think about the facets of Your character, I see how much I need to grow. I would ask You to help me today/this week to make progress in the following facets of holiness: [List one or more of God's character traits about which you feel a conviction.]

_____

_____

_____

Through the powerful name of Your Son, who makes it possible for me to be remade in Your image, amen.

CHAPTER 15

It's Time to Rebuild

*R*eceiving our true inheritance enables us to undertake the mighty work of rebuilding the church. This work of rebuilding can be better understood by looking at the example of Ezra, who was called by God to rebuild the temple in Jerusalem after the Babylonian captivity of the children of Israel. (See Ezra 1:1–7.)

Cyrus, the Persian ruler, had conquered Babylon nearly seventy years after the Israelites had been taken into captivity there, and he decreed that the temple in Jerusalem should be rebuilt. The effort was undertaken against many obstacles. Years later, King Darius renewed the decree of Cyrus, and he commissioned Ezra to complete the rebuilding.

God initiated the rebuilding of the temple by the power of His Spirit, much as He's doing today with the church. Just as the leaders rose up to undertake the task that Cyrus had decreed, today we see "spiritual fathers" rising up in the church.

The leaders had been in captivity for almost seventy years, but when it was time to build, they heard the voice of the Lord and got into position. They restored true worship according to the pattern of the tabernacle that God had originally revealed to Moses. After true worship was restored, the fear of the Lord came upon the people—and that started releasing everything else.

> And all the people shouted with a great shout when they praised the Lord, because the foundation of the house of the Lord was laid!
>
> —Ezra 3:11

True worship is built on the foundation of godly character, which flows from the Spirit of God to His people. God's pattern is to flow through anointed leadership, who impart the blessing to sons and daughters through example.

A great shaking is taking place in the body of Christ, and everyone must begin to serve according to the "measure of faith" God has given him or her. The Spirit of the Lord is bringing His house into order. The devil always tries to sabotage God's plan. He did in the days of Ezra's rebuilding, and he will in this day. But as the church comes into spiritual alignment, the Lord will literally take that which the enemy intends to harm God's people and use it for our benefit.

The rebuilders of God's temple refused to let go of their vision and their call—which was to rebuild tirelessly regardless of the objections and taunts of the enemy peoples around them—and they demonstrated the truth of Proverbs 16:7, "When a man's ways please the Lord, He makes even his enemies to be at peace with him." The pagan king Darius supplied everything they needed to worship God according to Moses' command.

In the same way, a spiritual leader imparts the sevenfold character to God into His people (their divine inheritance from the Lord), and their worship releases God's power and glory.

> He refreshes and restores my life (my self); He leads me in the paths of righteousness [uprightness and right standing with Him—not for my earning it, but] for His name's sake. Yes, though I walk through the [deep, sunless] valley of the shadow of death, I will fear or dread no evil, for You are with me; Your rod [to protect] and Your staff [to guide], they comfort me. You prepare a table before me in

the presence of my enemies. You anoint my head with oil; my [brimming] cup runs over.

—PSALM 23:3–5

Orphans

Do you have spiritual parents—or do you feel like a spiritual orphan? Read Acts 9, the story of Paul's first days as a Christian to see how God became "a father of the fatherless" (Ps. 68:5).

1.   For how many days after his conversion was Paul blind and without spiritual leadership or even fellowship? (In other words, how long was he a spiritual orphan [v. 9]?)

_____

2.   Speculate as to what he might have been thinking and feeling during this time:

_____

_____

_____

3.   Whom did God send to start the process of restoring Paul's sight and bringing him into the kingdom (vv. 10–19)?

_____

4.   Apparently, this believer went to see Paul alone. Who, therefore, can we assume baptized Paul?

_____

5.   Who else got involved in Paul's first days as a Christian (vv. 19–25)?

_____

6. Why did Paul leave them (v. 25)?

_____

7. How was he received in Jerusalem?

_____

8. Who took Paul "under his wing"?

_____

9. In your experience, can you cite an example of a time when someone reached out to you like that (or when you took care of someone else in that way)?

_____

_____

The Seven Attributes of True Worship

Each of the seven sacrificial elements that Darius restored to Israel give us a powerful revelation of how the Father's character operates in His sons and daughters:

- Young bulls
- Rams
- Lambs
- Wheat
- Salt
- Wine
- Oil

They must all work together, or the structure of our worship won't be stable. Let's take a look at each of these elements.

In the Old Testament tabernacle, a *young bull* (unblemished, a "first fruit") was sacrificed in the sin offering. In our lives, this is the same as a true son or daughter who always seeks to give the best to God, in purity. True sons and daughters are always willing to come to the altar and repent.

Two *rams* were also part of the sacrifice, one as a sweet savor unto the Lord and one for consecration. Sons and daughters of the kingdom willingly separate themselves to pray and make intercession for others. They are constantly drawn into His presence—and they always want more. The anointing on their lives is obvious.

Two *lambs* were sacrificed daily: one in the morning and one in the evening. Sons and daughters of the kingdom willingly take up their crosses and follow the Lord morning, noon, and night. Like a lamb, they are meek and obedient; they don't gossip, backbite, murmur, or complain against the Lord, but they follow Him (sacrificially) wherever He leads.

Wheat often speaks of provision and blessing. It also represents the harvest and the fat of the land. Even in sacrifice, the spirits of true sons and daughters rejoice in the Lord, and they are fruitful in the things of God.

Salt was rubbed onto the meat for every sacrifice. It not only enhanced the flavor, but it also symbolized loyalty and preservation. This corresponds to the way spiritual sons and daughters stand firm in covenant relationships with God and others, which makes them effective for His kingdom.

Both *wine* and *oil* go through a process of pressing. *Wine* was used in the sacrifices as a drink offering. Jesus used wine to represent His blood, and He talked about the "new wine" (Matt. 9:15–17). For a son or daughter of the gospel, the process of "pressing" in his or her life yields righteousness.

Oil represents the anointing of the Holy Spirit. Holy oil anointed all the tabernacle elements as well as the priests. Similarly, the anointing of a son or daughter of God is evident as they serve.

These seven sacrificial elements, which do not come by human strength but only by the Spirit of the Lord, confirm that sons and daughters of the kingdom have received their true inheritance.

As they stay in spiritual alignment, they continue to walk in their inheritance.

> Except the Lord builds the house, they labor in vain who build it; except the Lord keeps the city, the watchman wakes but in vain.

—PSALM 127:1

Getting Personal

I had been working hard in my church for years. Even though I was aware of the devil, he didn't usually seem to target me. Then things shifted. (I don't think I did anything wrong, but it's possible that I did.) Suddenly, everything I touched seemed to go bad, especially my relationships in the church. I found out later that I wasn't the only one having trouble, but at the time I felt like a leper.

It got so bad that I couldn't trust anyone. I couldn't function very well; I felt like I was half-paralyzed. It would have been easy to get angry and bitter—and it would have been a big relief to just "turn tail" and run. But something made me stay to see if things would improve. I fasted and prayed and looked around for signs of hope. I prayed for my pastor and the leadership of our church.

To my amazement, I began to hear rebuke and correction coming from the pulpit, much of which addressed the issues I had been dealing with. I was glad to see that my pastor wasn't afraid to talk about hard things. Nothing changed overnight, but eventually the atmosphere cleared. I came out of the "cave" I'd been hiding in.

I think in the future I'll be more attentive to keeping my walk as pure as possible and to appreciate and respect

> my spiritual covering. Now I understand about the church
> being like an outpost of heaven in enemy territory.
>
> —A. R.

The House of the Lord Will Be Completed

Spiritual alignment is being restored to the church, and things are shaking in the realm of the Spirit, because the kingdoms of the earth must become the kingdoms of our God and His Christ. We are in a powerful time of transition.

We see God's pattern for spiritual alignment in the sixth chapter of Ezra:

> The returned exiles kept the Passover on the fourteenth day of the first month. For the priests and the Levites had purified themselves together; all of them were clean. So they killed the Passover lamb for all the returned exiles, for their brother priests, and for themselves. It was eaten by the Israelites who had returned from exile and by all who had joined them and separated themselves from the pollutions of the peoples of the land to seek the Lord, the God of Israel. They kept the Feast of Unleavened Bread for seven days with joy, for the Lord had made them joyful and had turned the heart of the king of Assyria [referring to Darius king of Persia] to them, so that he strengthened their hands in the work of the house of God, the God of Israel.
>
> —Ezra 6:19–22

The priests purified themselves, and then the Israelites separated themselves to seek the Lord. The anointing flowed through proper spiritual alignment, and true worship was birthed in God's people.

To receive their spiritual inheritance and to act on it, leaders must obey the voice of the Father, and sons and daughters must honor leadership. The hearts of the fathers must return to the children and children must return to the fathers, or the blessings of God cannot be released in the earth.

Concluding Thought

I urge you to take to God in prayer every issue He has brought to the surface as you read this book. Decide today to become a son or daughter of the kingdom, obedient to the voice of your heavenly Father and submitted to those He has given you as spiritual covering here on earth. No devil can stop Him from leading you into your divine destiny—*but you can,* if you choose to ignore His voice.

He has chosen you, and He has given you the power to choose Him.

> ### The Essentials
>
> As we receive our true spiritual inheritance, which is characterized by godly character, we will be anointed to help rebuild the church and usher in the kingdom of God.

> ### Memory Verse
>
> His divine power has given us everything we need for life and godliness through our knowledge of him who called us by his own glory and goodness.
>
> —2 PETER 1:3, NIV

To Your Father

Dear heavenly Father, thank You for revealing the truth about my spiritual inheritance. Forgive me for the times I have removed myself from Your covering by disobeying

Your Word or failing to acknowledge the counsel of my spiritual parents. I now know that in their counsel I will find true riches.

Father, I acknowledge my sin; cleanse me from all unrighteousness, and help me to become a true son/daughter of the gospel. Create in me a clean heart, and renew a right spirit within me.

Thank You, Lord, that I can hear Your voice, obey the counsel of Your Word, and activate the full measure of faith You've placed in my spirit. From this day forward, I thank You for helping me to become a true servant in Your kingdom. Amen.

If you make this your daily prayer and remember the Word of the Lord, your foundation in the Spirit will be strong. I'm standing before God with you.

Submitted to His Word,
Juanita Bynum

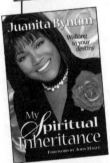

Strang Communications, the publisher of both Charisma House and *Charisma* magazine, wants to give you 3 FREE ISSUES of our award-winning magazine.

Since its inception in 1975, *Charisma* magazine has helped thousands of Christians stay connected with what God is doing worldwide.

Within its pages you will discover in-depth reports and the latest news from a Christian perspective, biblical health tips, global events in the body of Christ, personality profiles, and so much more. Join the family of *Charisma* readers who enjoy feeding their spirit each month with miracle-filled testimonies and inspiring articles that bring clarity, provoke prayer, and demand answers.

To claim your **3 free issues** of *Charisma,* send your name and address to: Charisma 3 Free Issue Offer, 600 Rinehart Road, Lake Mary, FL 32746. Or you may call 1-800-829-3346 and ask for Offer # 93FREE. This offer is only valid in the USA.

---

www.charismamag.com